ISLAM: Path of Infinite Love

Guide to Cultivating Inner Peace and Mindful Living

Dr. Eeshat Ansari

This book is one of three thematic volumes derived from the author's earlier and more comprehensive publication, *The Purest Monotheism: Monotheistic Islam, Polytheistic Muslims*. The thematic division was intended to improve readability and make the material easier for readers to follow.

The present volume focuses on the theme of unconditional love. Some sections of *Islam: Path of Infinite Love* are newly written, while many others are adapted from the original work.

ISLAM: PATH OF INFINITE LOVE
Fourth Edition
Copyright © Eeshat Ansari 2025, 2020, 2018, 2017, 2016, 2014
eeshat11@yahoo.com

	eBook	Paperback	Hardback
ISBN	979-8-9923961-1-9	979-8-9923961-2-6	979-8-9923961-3-3

Dedicated to

My Mother and Father
Whom I remember as
Ammi and Abba

They taught me how to love,
how to think and find the truth,
and how to have the courage to say what is true.

**My Lord! Have mercy on them (parents) as they cared for
me when I was little** [17:24]

Table of Contents

CHAPTER 1

LOVING ALLAH UNCONDITIONALLY

Wherever you are and whatever you do, be in love
~ Rumi

Persian Sufi poet Attar of Nishapur (died- 1221 CE) said:

Let love lead your soul.
Make it a place to retire to,
a kind of monastery cave,
a retreat for the deepest core of your being.[1]

Discover something truly amazing when you learn to love Allah *unconditionally*. This love can unlock a universe of blessings and contentment beyond imagination. Allow yourself to experience the transformative power of pure, selfless, and unconditional love. Embrace it with an open heart and mind, and watch as it brings a newfound sense of purpose, depth, and meaning to your life. The unconditional love of Allah is like a soothing fragrance that spreads peace and joy around you. It brings you closer to Allah and helps you find solace and strength in Him. Medieval Islamic jurisconsult and theologian Ibn Qayyim al-Jawziyya explains love as:

The very spirit of Islam, the pivotal point of religion and the axis of [eternal] happiness and deliverance.[2]

It is literally impossible to imagine spiritual Islam without love.

Once, Muslim Sufi Rabia Basri was asked, "Do you love Allah?"
She answered yes.
"Do you hate the devil?"
She answered,
"My love for Allah leaves me no time to hate the devil." [3]

1

Rabia's love for Allah was uninterrupted, unconditional, beautiful, and infinite. Love engulfed her every single moment and entire existence. Loving Allah takes a believer to the highest form of spiritual ecstasy. On the other hand, hating anyone causes suffering to one's own self. There was no reason for Rabia to take time away from everlasting bliss just to hate the devil. Was there?

Rabia's above quote carries two important messages. First, loving Allah can offer unparalleled spiritual contentment and satisfaction. The second message is that the *feeling of peace and happiness from loving Allah can be maintained without interruption*. Rabia was not the only one who experienced *continuous* ecstasy of divine love and peace. Her story resonates with hundreds of Sufis throughout history. For example, Rumi said:

> Laugh as much as you breathe. Love as long as you live.[4]

EACH OF US WOULD LIKE TO LOVE SOMEONE AND BE LOVED

Infants require more than just nourishment and clothing to thrive - they also crave love and affection. The care and attention given to them during these early years can significantly impact their growth and development. Psychology Professor Fredrickson states, "Children who have early loving relationships with their parents grow up to be more compassionate adults."[5]

On the other hand, the lack of love can have a significantly adverse effect. According to author Dr. David Hamilton, "If an infant is born into an environment lacking in love, emotional warmth, and responsiveness, the growth of its brain is hugely affected."[6]

The craving for love is a universal and lifelong dependency. French novelist George Sand (1804-1876) said, "There is only one happiness in life, to love and be loved."[7] This is one of the undeniable realities of life. We like to be loved, and at the same time, we want to love someone wholeheartedly. How do we achieve these two goals? The good news is that Islam provides guidance.

Unconditional love can transform a person's mental and physical state. According to Sufi scholar Vaughan-Lee, "The power of love takes the Sufi wayfarer beyond the mind and the ego into the arena of the heart.

Love is the fire that burns and transforms the lover, causing both bewilderment and intoxication, freeing the lover from everything but God."[8]

Rumi said,

> Love is the water of life, jump into this water.[9]

WHAT IS LOVE: ACTION OR FEELING?

Love is only a feeling or an emotion. That is it. Love is *not* an action. Sometimes, love can inspire an action. Stated differently, love and action can exist simultaneously. Consider when a loving mother gives water to her thirsty baby. Here, the mother loves the child, and the inspired act is giving water to the baby. In other words, the mother's love is manifested by the act of giving water to the baby. It not only quenches the baby's thirst but also provides a sense of security, comfort, and nurturing that is essential for the baby's emotional and physical development. Conversely, an action alone does not necessarily prove that love exists. The same physical action may be performed without love. If a babysitter gives water to a baby without emotions, then even though the action is identical, love is not involved.

Rabia said:

> In love between heart and heart.
> Speech is born out of longing,
> True description from the real taste.
> The one who tastes, knows;
> the one who explains, lies.[10]

It is impossible for human language to describe how one feels when one loves Allah unconditionally. To learn how to swim, you need to get into the water and not just read a book. Loving Allah unconditionally is the foundation of experiencing the true essence of Islam. A great deal of Sufi literature, accumulated over centuries, proves that it is not only possible for a person to love Allah, but it is the most satisfying human spiritual experience. When you embrace this love, your heart will be filled with the purest form of compassion and devotion. Allah's love is already embedded in our hearts. Rumi recommends:

> The inspiration you seek is already within you. Be silent and listen.[11]

The Quran says: **"My Lord is indeed *Merciful, Loving"*** (11:90). This verse uses two names or attributes of Allah together: the Merciful and the Loving. Allah is loving, and His love is manifested by His mercy.

The Quran has several verses in which Allah reminds us of His infinite mercy, which, as the above verse suggests, coexists with love. The Quran asks: **"Who sends down rainwater from the sky and in addition to that produces vegetation of all kinds: He [Allah] brings forth green crops ... gardens of grapes, olives, and pomegranates...In these things, *there are signs* for true believers"** (6:99). A true believer not only thanks Allah for His mercy *but also feels the love of Allah.* Love takes the believer closer to Allah. Sufi Rabia said:

My Beloved is always with me.[12]

WHO CREATED LOVE?

Allah is the one and only God. Therefore, Allah is the only Creator there can be. The Quran mentions explicitly that the beautiful gifts of love and kindness are also from Allah: **"He [Allah] created love and kindness in your hearts"** (30:21). Love and kindness inspire us to be supportive and helpful to others.

Allah also gave humans the capability to choose. It is a tragedy when people choose to spread hate instead of love. Let us choose love, a special gift from Allah, over hate and create a kinder, more compassionate, and more accepting world. Spreading positivity through small gestures can profoundly impact someone's life. Whether it is a smile, a kind word, or a simple act of generosity, each act of love can create ripples of compassion and build a more harmonious world.

WHO GAVE HUMANS THE CAPABILITY TO LIVE IN A SOCIETY?

Allah also gave humans the capability to form social groups. Before Prophet Muhammad[PBUH] (superscript PBUH stands for *peace be upon him*) migrated to Medina, two Medina tribes, Aus and Khazraj, were sworn enemies. At that time, Arab tribes took pride in taking revenge, and inter-tribal wars could last for generations. However, after Prophet Muhammad[PBUH] migrated to Medina, by the blessing of Allah, the Prophet[PBUH] made peace between these tribes. In the Quran, Allah reminds the members of the tribes: **"Remember Allah's favors upon you when you were enemies; He brought your *hearts together,* you became, by**

His favor, brothers" (3:103). The history of early Muslims is a testament to their selfless love and compassion for one another. For instance, early Muslims in Medina generously opened their homes to accommodate the emigrants from Mecca, providing them shelter, food, and support. Their actions and deeds truly reflected the values they held dear. In addition to prioritizing their relationships, they fostered an environment of care and support.

The following poignant story highlights the deep bond between the companions and demonstrates their profound care for each other (Companions or *Sahaba* were the Muslim contemporaries who saw or met the Prophet[PBUH]).

After the battle of Yarmouk was over, three companions, Al-Harith ibn Hisham, Ikrimah ibn Abi Jahl, and Ayyash ibn Abi Rabiah, were critically wounded on the battlefield. When the water was brought to Al-Harith, instead of drinking it himself, he asked that the water be given to his injured friend Ikrimah first. When the water was brought to Ikrimah, he pointed to another wounded companion, Ayyash. By the time the water reached Ayyash, he had passed away. By the time water was brought back to Ikrimah, he had also passed away. Finally, Al-Harith also died before drinking water. All three died, preferring their friends over themselves. The companions who witnessed this incident prayed that God may be pleased with them all and grant them refreshment from the spring of Kawthar in Paradise, a refreshment after which there is no more thirst.[13] This act of selflessness and sacrifice served as a reminder of the strong bond of friendship they shared. It prompted everyone to be more compassionate and considerate, emphasizing that life is not always about ourselves.

IS LOVE IDENTICAL TO SEX?

Islam makes an amazingly subtle distinction between love and sex, even if the emotion of love and the action of sex can exist simultaneously.

Fasting Believers are not allowed to drink, eat, or engage in sex from sunrise to sunset. While fasting, does Islam allow love between spouses? *During the fast, even if sex and lust are prohibited, love is permitted.*

A young man and an old man asked Prophet Muhammad[PBUH] if a fasting man is allowed to embrace his wife. Prophet Muhammad[PBUH] prohibited the young man. However, the Prophet's[PBUH] prophetic judgment determined that the old man would only embrace his wife out of love, not

5

lust. So, the Prophet[PBUH] permitted the old man to embrace his wife.[14] One word of caution: if the embrace leads to the emotion of lust, then Allah will know, and the fast will be broken.

WHOM SHOULD WE LOVE?

When it comes to the question of who to love, one school of thought teaches that we should shun this world because love and attachment to the world are considered hindrances to worship and spiritual growth.

Islam provides a balanced approach. It allows a Muslim to pursue worldly endeavors, earn an honest living, get married, and have family and friends. Naturally, we love the people, animals, and even objects that please, help, and benefit us.

However, priority plays an essential role. According to the Quran, a Muslim should love Allah and the Prophet[PBUH] more than any worldly possession (9:24). After all, the Prophet[PBUH] brought us the message of Allah and was especially blessed by Allah. The Quran tells the Prophet[PBUH], **"Allah has sent down to you the Book and wisdom and has taught you that which you did not know. Certainly, God's favor to you has been great."** (4:113).

Regarding the top priority, The Quran says: **"Some people consider certain things equal to God and love them just as one should love God. However, the strongest of the believers' love is their love of Allah"** (2:165). Undoubtedly, *we should have maximum love for Allah,* our creator, protector, sustainer, helper, and provider. The love of Allah is naturally ingrained in our hearts; all we have to do is tune into it. Rumi said:

> Your task is not to seek for love, but merely to seek and find all the barriers within yourself that you have built against it.[15]

The requirement that believers should have maximum love for Allah closely binds Islamic spiritual growth to unconditional love. It is the key to unraveling the secrets of faith and acquiring true inner peace and tranquility. Loving Allah unconditionally is the highest form of love that a human can attain.

LOVE CANNOT BE FORCED

The renowned Urdu poet Ghalib said:

> Love is like an uncontrollable fire,
> impossible to ignite or extinguish by force.

Love happens naturally, as if all by itself, in an environment of total freedom. A mother is not paid or forced to love her child, yet she does. Coercion, manipulation, and compulsion can never create love. A robber can rob a bank at gunpoint, but no one can be forced to love at gunpoint. It just does not work that way.

Love cannot be forced through willpower or regulated by a strict schedule. For example, you cannot say I will love my spouse from 12:05 PM to 3:47 PM on alternate Thursdays. Since loving Allah and loving humankind are essential parts of Islam, *it is impossible to impose Islam by force.* The Quran clearly explains, **"There is no compulsion in religion"** (2:256). The reason is that compulsion never creates love, whereas Islam cannot exist in a heart that lacks love. Why? Because believers should possess the utmost love for Allah, as stated in the verse, **"The strongest of the believers' love is their love of Allah"** (2:165). *Love is the cornerstone of Islamic belief, fostering a genuine connection between Allah and believers.*

Loving Allah is a very private feeling. Instead of forcing love, let the *love* pull and guide you. Rumi said:

> Let yourself be silently drawn
> by the strange pull of what you really love.
> It will not lead you astray.[16]

CONDITIONAL LOVE VS. UNCONDITIONAL LOVE

Conditional love is like a cold, distant, and impersonal business transaction. A person has to fulfill the conditions or expectations of the other person and only then receives compensation in the form of conditional love. It is similar to when you deposit a coin in a vending machine; you expect it to dispense a can of soda. If expectations are not met, then conditional love is immediately put on hold.

Suppose you spent lots of energy and money on your best friend's last birthday. In response, you were expecting your friend to return the favor. Instead, your friend even forgot your birthday. For sure, your expectations were not met, and your feelings would be hurt.

If your love is *unconditional,* you do not need to hold back the natural flowing love just because your friend forgot your birthday; therefore, you do not have to hold onto the memory of emotional pain. As a result, the suffering is significantly reduced. Also, in the absence of suffering, your wisdom is fully functional, allowing you to think of the most appropriate response. An individual with emotional maturity can accept both favorable and unfavorable situations. Cultivating emotional flexibility can help us navigate the ups and downs of life with greater ease while maintaining a positive outlook and unwavering faith in the Almighty's plan.

But if your love is conditional, to *get even,* you may hold back your love. You hold onto painful memories to justify the restriction you have placed on your love. Therefore, it is harder to get over the pain; this prolongs the suffering. Your wisdom will be clouded, and your response may be out of proportion. Conditional love is often based on a person's performance rather than on who they are as a person.

Conditional love also influences our social lives. Every person around you has to qualify to earn your love. Precious personal relationships are reduced to haggling over sales, like, 'I bought you a $50 jacket last year, and you only sent me a cheap New Year's card!'

To people with conditional love, lasting love seems an impossible goal, with the risk of heartbreak. They are afraid to hear or say, "I love you." Such preconditions complicate love beyond recognition. When two people interact over an extended period, it is natural to have disagreements and conflicts of interest. Such clashes can influence relationships. Even best friends, couples, siblings, and parents and children have arguments. If the love between them is merely conditional, then, sooner or later, many relationships will be severed, hearts will be broken, and only sour memories will be left behind.

ISLAM TEACHES UNCONDITIONAL LOVE

In contrast, the unconditional love of Islam has nothing to do with the behavior of others. A Muslim should continuously love others, regardless of what others do or believe.

A desert Arab came to meet Prophet Muhammad[PBUH] in the Al-Masjid an-Nabawi, which is regarded as the second-holiest mosque in Islam. When the desert Arab felt the need, he started urinating in one corner of the mosque. Prophet's companions tried to stop him, but Prophet Muhammad[PBUH] told them to let the desert Arab finish.

Later, very lovingly, Prophet Muhammad[PBUH] said to him, "These mosques are not the places meant for urine and filth, but are only for the remembrance of Allah, prayer, and the recitation of the Quran."[17]

Later, the area was washed clean with water. This incident is a beautiful example of unconditional love. Prophet Muhammad[PBUH] did not order punishment, even if it may have been justified. He did not humiliate the desert Arab either. When that desert Arab lived with city Muslims and learned their traditions, he openly expressed his surprise and gratitude that the Prophet[PBUH] did not reprimand or insult him after such a grievous mistake.[18] Instead, the Prophet[PBUH] accepted him the way he was and treated him with respect and kindness. What a beautiful example of unconditional love!

However, unconditional love does not mean you grin and bear it all or refrain from saying your side of the story. Prophet Muhammad[PBUH] tactfully and lovingly conveyed exactly *what he wanted to say*. Thus, unconditional love can be practiced in real life. It is worth noting that Prophet Muhammad[PBUH] also explained the *reason* why the sanctity of the mosque must be preserved. His response was calm and *logical*.

When we love unconditionally, *we can still say no without guilt*. If a child tries to stick a finger in an electric socket, the mother will say no and still love the child unconditionally.

What if someone crosses all reasonable limits of ethics and, without any justification, physically attacks you? *Loving unconditionally does not mean living in a make-believe world.* Islam provides realistic and practical solutions. In case one is attacked without any justification and negotiation is not possible, then Islam allows fighting back *in defense*.

On rare occasions, even some Prophets of Allah (sent before Prophet Muhammad[PBUH]) prayed against their oppressors, as in the case of Prophet Noah (26:117-118).

> **NOTE**: Islam is not a new religion. The very first human, Adam, was a Prophet of Islam. The Quran says: "**O Prophet [Muhammad[PBUH]], Allah have sent many messengers before you**" (40:78). Allah also gave holy books to some Prophets. The Quran says: "**Allah sent down the Taurat (Torah) and the Injeel (Gospel)**" (3:3). Muslims believe that

parts of the old books (before the Quran) have been corrupted or lost. All Prophets, including Prophets Abraham[PBUH] and Noah[PBUH], preached pure monotheism.

At the same time, do not make demands that are beyond the capability of others. Prophet Muhammad[PBUH] let the desert Arab finish urinating because, once started, the process cannot be immediately interrupted. The best part of unconditional love is that one's heart is always free from hate and anger. We must love others continuously, regardless of how they behave toward us. A good example is a mother's love for her newborn. This love does not diminish, even if the baby cries or keeps the mother awake at night. Rumi said,

> Whenever we manage to love without expectations, calculations, or negotiations, we are indeed in heaven.[19]

Here is one more example. At-Tufayl ibn Amr was the leader of the Daws tribe. The people of his tribe respected and obeyed him. He learned Islam from Prophet Muhammad[PBUH] and converted. He was very confident that, if he asked, the tribe members would also convert to Islam. However, to his disappointment, the tribe refused.

Disheartened, At-Tufayl went to Prophet Muhammad[PBUH] and complained about his tribe. After hearing him, Prophet Muhammad[PBUH] raised his hand to pray. The onlookers thought that the Prophet[PBUH] might put a curse on the tribe. Instead, the Prophet[PBUH] prayed, "O Lord, guide [the tribe of] Daws."[20] He prayed to Allah to bless the members of the Daws tribe with the guidance of Islam. Such individuals will attain paradise, which is the ultimate human achievement. Even if the people of Daws were not Muslims, the Prophet[PBUH] prayed for them. In the context of cursing the polytheists, the Prophet[PBUH] pointed out, "I have not been sent as the invoker of the curse, but I have been sent as a mercy [to the worlds as explained in verse (21:107)]."[21] The Prophet's[PBUH] comments about the tribe of Daws also prove that Muslims should unconditionally love *all humanity,* not just Muslims.

Unconditional love in Islam is not just the discipline of one's emotions. Instead, it is a *sincere concern* for everyone. Even though we may hold different religious beliefs, we can still work together to make this world a better place. Only then can we create a peaceful and harmonious society for ourselves and future generations.

Rumi describes unconditional love as,

> The garden of love is green without limit
> and yields many fruits other than sorrow or joy.
> Love is beyond either condition:
> without spring, without autumn, it is always fresh.[22]

THE ONE EXCEPTION

We discussed above that even if you love someone unconditionally, you still have the right to say no. Is a person also allowed to say no to Allah's commands as well? According to the Quran, a Muslim cannot refuse Allah's commands. Since Prophet Muhammad[PBUH] gave us the message of Allah; therefore, a Muslim must obey both the Quran and the hadith: **"Tell the people O Muhammad[PBUH]: 'If you sincerely love Allah, then follow me'"** (3:31).

The term *hadith* (plural: *ahadith*) is defined as: "The traditions relating to the deeds and utterances of the prophet as recounted by the companions."[23] This includes the tacit approvals or disapprovals by Prophet Muhammad[PBUH]. The hadith collection also includes the actions and words of the four guided Caliphs because they were highly knowledgeable about Islam.

Obeying Allah without questioning is not an unfair requirement because the Quran assures us that **"Allah does not burden any human being with more than he can bear"** (2:286). It means that every command of Allah is designed not to exceed our endurance abilities.

The above verse 3:31 also recommends that obedience to Allah should be motivated by love instead of other minor motives, like duty, discipline, or habit.

IS IT ALLOWED TO USE UNCONDITIONAL LOVE TO ASK FOR ALLAH'S FAVORS?

Many prayers in the Quran describe various reasons for seeking Allah's help. For example, Prophet Moses[PBUH] used his helplessness as an excuse to seek Allah's help: **"O Lord! Surely, I am in desperate need of whatever good that You may send down to me"** (28:24). In another prayer, Prophet Zakariyah[PBUH] used the weakness of his old age: **"O Lord! Surely my bones have weakened, and the hair of my head glistens with gray, ... grant me an heir by Your grace"** (19:4–5). *But not a single* *prayer in the Quran uses love as leverage to gain Allah's favor.* No prayer says, 'Allah, help me because I love you.' That is because Islam advocates *unconditional* love, a special gift from Allah. Consider the unconditional love a mother feels for her newborn child.

If a person attempts to barter love in exchange for Allah's favor, the fundamental virtue of *unconditionality* is violated. Love is being downgraded to the level of a haggling business transaction. This diminishes its worth and goes against its very essence. *No wonder you cannot find a prayer in the Quran that uses love as currency or a bargaining chip to ask for Allah's favor.*

Interestingly, the Quran beautifully and *consistently* preserves the inherent virtue and purity of unconditional love in all areas. It is impossible for humans to imagine such abstract concepts. *This serves as further proof that the Quran is a divinely inspired book.*

UNDERSTANDING 'LOVE FOR ALLAH'

The Quran *directly orders* believers to perform various worship rituals. **"Be steadfast in prayer; practice regular charity"** (2:43). When it comes to love, the Quran only mentions the *characteristic* of believers, **"The strongest of the believers' love is their love of Allah"** (2:165). It is noteworthy that, unlike the worship rituals, the Quran does *not* explicitly instruct believers to love Allah. Why? Because Allah created the emotion of love. Allah also gave love the limitation that love cannot be forced. Any specific command to love Allah would have violated the very nature of love! That would be an impossible instruction. Here, we see yet another evidence that the Quran is the book of God.

The above verse (2:165) does not say that believers should only love Allah and no one else. Instead, believers are allowed to love others, though their utmost love should be for Allah alone. This does not mean that if a mother loves her child, she should try to set a fixed quota for the child's love and transfer the remaining love to Allah.

A Muslim mother of a newborn realizes that her existence is not a coincidence. Allah is the one who gave her life. Her every heartbeat and breath are a gift from generous and loving Allah. When she appreciates the beauty of the bright, oversized rainbow on the horizon, the happy movement of red flowers when washed clean by raindrops, or peaceful, aimlessly floating seagulls in a nippy ocean breeze, she thanks Allah for beautiful gifts of nature and loves Allah. In her gratitude, she also appreciates that Allah loves her and has bestowed upon her countless blessings.

She knows that Allah is the only One who created love and put love in the hearts of humankind. Therefore, all the love she ever received from her parents, siblings, other relatives, spouse, children, friends, and pets is a manifestation of Allah's love for her. She prays: **"My Lord! Grant me the grace that *I may thank you* for the favors which You have bestowed on me and my parents"** (46:15). Her precious child is not a coincidence either, but the most cherished gift of love from Allah. She thanks Allah for the gift of her child. With this understanding, she naturally ends up unconditionally loving Allah the *most*.

This does not mean that loving Allah is yet another burdensome responsibility. Discovering how to love Allah unlocks a deeper level of love within us. When we love Allah unconditionally, we also end up unconditionally loving His creation, including the entirety of humankind. By nourishing and cherishing this love, we spread positivity, compassion, and kindness wherever we go. This is the most enlightening thing one can do for spiritual and emotional growth. This love fills every moment of our lives with beauty, peace, and happiness. Sufi Attar said:

> The whole world is a marketplace for Love,
> For naught that is, from Love remains remote.
> The Eternal Wisdom made all things in Love.
> On Love they all depend, to Love all turn.
> The Earth, the Heavens, the sun, the moon, the stars
> The center of their orbit is found in Love.
> By Love, are all bewildered, stupefied,
> Intoxicated by the Wine of Love.[24]

WHAT CAN WE DO TO EARN ALLAH'S LOVE?

The Quran defines how a believer may earn Allah's love. Allah encourages generous behavior toward humanity by explicitly saying that Allah *loves* those who give to charity (3:134), who are patient in adversity (3:146), who do good deeds (2:195), and who seek forgiveness for sins (2:222).

Wherever *possible*, believers should try to remain kind even when others mistreat them. Allah ordains a general principle: **"*Repel other's evil deeds with your good deeds.* You will see that he with whom you had enmity will become your close friend"** (41:34) (also see exceptional case under the above heading "Islam Teaches Unconditional Love").

13

Mercy and Unconditional Love for Allah's Creation

How should believers behave towards Allah's other creatures? The Prophet[PBUH] recounted an incident involving a prostitute who encountered a panting stray dog near a well, on the brink of dying from thirst. She did not have anything available to get water from the well. So, she took off her shoe, tied it to her head scarf, and drew some water from the well to give to the dog. The Prophet[PBUH] continued, "So, Allah forgave her because of that."[25]

Notably, she did not make all the effort to gain recognition, power, or money. Her only motive was unconditional love. This proves believers should be compassionate and generous towards Allah's other creatures. It is another way to earn Allah's love. No wonder Allah rewarded her.

ALLAH FORGIVES YOU AND LOVES YOU

The Quran says, "He [Allah] is the All-forgiving, the Most Loving One" (85:14). Again, two names of Allah, the Forgiving and the Loving, come together. Allah's love is expressed through His act of forgiveness.

Individuals may think I have committed too many sins; therefore, Allah would not love me. The thoughtful perception of the above verse removes this common roadblock by reminding believers that Allah is *all-forgiving*. Next, the verse mentions the attribute 'the Most Loving.' It means that Allah, *who forgives, loves you*. How can any believer find an excuse to deny Allah's love?

Allah says, **"O My servants [a very loving Arabic term used here] who have transgressed against their souls,** *do not despair of Allah's mercy*, **for Allah forgives all sins. It is He Who is the Forgiving, the Merciful"** (39:53).

There are many examples of Allah's forgiveness and mercy. Here is one instance: Muslims bury their deceased instead of cremating them. One Muslim sinner was so concerned about his sins that, before his death, he directed his sons to cremate him and scatter his ashes into the sea. As a result, he hoped that Allah would not be able to re-create his body. Thus, he hoped to escape Allah's punishment. After he died, his sons cremated him. Later, Allah, the omnipotent, recreated his body and asked the man why he preferred cremation. The man confessed to his plan to evade Allah's punishment. In response, *Allah forgave him.*[26]

14

Notably, the man was a sinner, but he did not ask any intermediary, prophet, deceased saint, angel, god, or goddess to save him. He was afraid of Allah *only* and no other deity or human. The man firmly believed in *la ilaha il-Allah*, or 'no god exists other than Allah.' The man also believed that Allah's punishment was real. Though he was a sinner, he still completely fulfilled the agreement he made with Allah alongside all human souls to worship Allah only, as described in the Quran (7:172). No wonder the Merciful, the Forgiving, the Loving Allah forgave this man.

Here is another example of Allah's forgiveness. In the Battle of Uhud, Prophet Muhammad[PBUH] assigned 70 Muslim archers to guard against a surprise attack from pagan forces behind the Muslim army. He gave strict orders to the archers *not to leave their posts under any circumstances.*

Early in the battle, the Muslims started to win, and the pagan army fled. After that, the Muslim army followed the centuries-old Arab tradition of looting war booty (later, this practice was prohibited). At that time, many archers disobeyed the Prophet and joined the looters. As a result, the back of the Muslim army was no longer adequately protected. Pagans used this opportunity to attack Muslims from behind their lines. Consequently, many Muslims died. Several Muslims, including the Prophet[PBUH], were injured. Even by today's military standards, such gross disobedience to a commanding officer would warrant severe punishment. Instead, Allah commanded the Prophet[PBUH] to forgive the archers for their negligent and reckless behavior. Allah instructed the Prophet[PBUH] to pray for the forgiveness of the archers and to consult them on various matters, just as he did with the other believers, and not to cast them aside: **"*Pardon* them [the disobedient archers] and *ask Allah's forgiveness* for them. Consult them in the conduct of affairs"** (3:159). Honestly, can a human being be so generous?

The Quran says that: **"He [Allah] is All-forgiving and All-merciful"** (12:98). All a Muslim has to do is *sincerely* seek forgiveness. The Quran also prohibits hopelessness and despair. **"Never give up hope of Allah's mercy"** (12:87). Any Muslim who gives up hope of forgiveness from Allah has the wrong concept of Allah.

According to Sufi Poet Sultan Bahu:

> The river of oneness has surged,
> quenching the thirst of the deserts and wastelands.
> If you don't nurture God's love in your heart,
> you will be dry and parched like those deserts.[27]

15

However, there is only one sin that Allah will never forgive—if a person *dies* with polytheistic beliefs. The only solution is that during earthly life, a polytheist should repent to Allah and believe in Islamic monotheism. They should also live a life of piety and charity. This critical problem and its solution are discussed in the author's other book, '*The Purest Monotheism: Monotheistic Islam. Polytheistic Muslims.*' The description of this book can be found in Appendix B.

HOW CAN WE HAVE THE UTMOST LOVE FOR ALLAH?

The yearning for unconditional love is a universal human desire. We all crave to be loved unconditionally and, in turn, to love someone in the same way. But how can we achieve this?

When You Feel the Need to Love Someone

Who can we love all the time, day or night, in every situation (even in the midst of *major crises)?* Who truly appreciates our love and care? Who can always offer us the best emotional support, and who is not imaginary but real? The answer to these questions is simple: *Love Allah.*

Loving Allah is not a complex task but a natural inclination that we can nurture and develop. We know that love cannot be compelled by determination or willpower. This leads to a difficult paradox: *What is the practical way to love Allah without using compulsion?*

We can get the answer by closely analyzing the verse: **"The strongest of the <u>believers'</u> love is their love of Allah"** (2:165). This verse, with its profound wisdom, not only tells us to have ultimate love for Allah but also teaches us that Allah's love is the *consequence of having good Islamic belief.* We cannot use self-control or willpower to cultivate love, but we can strive to have steadfast faith (or become better Muslims), and consequently, we will end up loving Allah the most.

Another feature of verse (2:165) is that it *gently* reminds us that believers are supposed to have maximum love for Allah. The beauty of this verse is it does *not directly demand* love. Nevertheless, the message to love Allah to the fullest is as clear as daylight. All we have to do is to *repeatedly* recite: **"The strongest of the believers' love is their love of Allah"** (2:165). As a result, the verse serves as a gentle reminder without putting any pressure. *This is a stress-free way to guide us toward embracing the unconditional love of Allah.* Does it work? Of course, it does. Simply recite the above verse repeatedly, either aloud or silently, and observe the outcome.

Unconditional love is the very foundation of the Islamic faith. It is the bond that connects us to our Creator, making us feel a part of something greater. It is the highest form of worship and the only way to experience true peace and contentment. Staying faithful to the divine objective of loving Allah helps us stay focused on our spiritual journey.

When You Wish to Be Loved

To feel Allah's love repeatedly, recite: "**He [Allah] is the All-forgiving, the Most Loving One**" (85:14). If anyone doubts that sins will prevent Allah's love, then as*k for Allah's forgiveness* and then repeatedly recite the verse (85:14).

As a result, you may even feel divine guidance helping you stay on track. Your journey may lead you to unexpected opportunities and moments of clarity.

Two-way Loving Bond with Allah

Consider the beautiful example of the mother and newborn. Allah has blessed the mother with unconditional love for her newborn, and in return, the infant loves the mother unconditionally. However, the most precious moments are when the mother and child love each other *simultaneously*, creating a harmonious connection.

Similarly, verse (2:165) tells us that Allah has blessed the believers with the capacity to have maximum love for Him. When embraced, divine love becomes a guiding force that brings harmony and tranquility to our lives and enriches our spiritual journey.

In the ideal case, the believers do not just love Allah; simultaneously, they also feel the profound love from their Creator, as in verse (85:14). This experience of feeling Allah's love is not just a fleeting emotion but a deep and profound connection that allows us to experience a sense of spiritual fulfillment that is beyond words.

Let us all strive to love Allah and simultaneously feel His love.

17

Allah is always close to you. The Quran says: **"We know [Allah knows] what his [human's] soul whispers to him. We are closer to him than even his jugular vein"** (50:16). Allah fully understands you and values

your love. He is always there for you, even when you are unaware. He is always there to comfort you in times of need and provide answers and guidance. He is your best friend and supporter.

It should be noted that in the above verse (12:22), Allah uses the pronoun 'We' instead of 'I' for Himself. Several languages, like Arabic, English, Urdu, and Hindi,[28] allow using the *majestic plural*, where the plural pronoun refers to a single person holding an important position. Such usage in English is called the "royal we."[29] For example: *We, the king of England.*

To love Allah the most, practice the following two steps:

PRACTICAL STEP 1: Embark on your spiritual journey to cultivate maximum love for Allah by repeatedly reciting the above verses (2:165) or (85:14), either using your tongue or silently in your heart. For the best results, memorize these verses in Arabic. As you do this frequently, you will feel the transformative power of this practice.

PRACTICAL STEP 2: To make steady progress on the path of love, as advised by verse 2:165, *strive to strengthen your faith*. How? We should try to engage in regular prayers, fasting, charity, performing Hajj, reciting the Quran, serving humanity, showing gratitude to Allah, and being thankful to Him. The subject will be discussed in more detail later in the book. These are powerful ways to deepen your love for Allah.

UNCONDITIONALLY LOVING YOURSELF

The Quran praises those who achieve complete inner peace and contentment. Such individuals are described as possessing *Nafs-e-Mutma'inna*. Allah promises them Paradise (Quran 89:27). To reach the level of *Nafs-e-Mutma'inna,* you must also learn to *love yourself unconditionally.* Loving yourself unconditionally allows you to forgive yourself, respect yourself, and be kind to yourself. You do not set unrealistic goals for yourself. It leads you to happiness and contentment. Self-love is also the foundation for meaningful relationships with others. If you hold back from loving yourself (or love yourself conditionally), then, as a rule of thumb, you can never become a fully satisfied person.

Please recall that believers are supposed to have maximum love for Allah. This can only be realized if a believer creates a two-way loving bond based on the understanding that Allah loves the believer, and the believer loves Allah.

If you do not love yourself, you will compulsively deny love from other humans. Such a person will be in a state of spiritual stagnation and will not feel love even from Allah. Consequently, it is impossible to have maximum love for Allah. The solution is to learn how to love oneself *unconditionally*. The following paragraph explains how to achieve this goal.

Start by loving Allah the most, as described in the previous section, by repeatedly reciting verses (2:165) or (85:14), either using your tongue or silently in your heart. Soon, you will reach a stage where you will feel a deep-rooted state of self-worth and happiness. You will realize that you are much more valuable than you previously believed. That will also open the door to loving yourself unconditionally, *in sha Allah* (if Allah wills). Rumi said:

> You are more precious than both heaven and Earth;
> What can I [say] more?
> You know not your own worth
> You know not your own worth.
> Sell not yourself at little price,
> Being so precious in Allah's eyes.[30]

However, *loving yourself* should always be done in the Islamic way. Regarding personal achievements and possessions, we should give full credit only to Allah and not to ourselves because Allah is the only source of our successes and achievements. Everything we possess belongs to Allah. Even our bodies are not our own but belong to Allah: **"To Him belongs all that is in the Heavens and the Earth"** (2:255). A good Muslim constantly thanks Allah for His mercy, seeks His forgiveness, and generously donates to charity. Such a person is polite, humble, and kind to others. Unconditional love never leads to arrogance, egotism, or narcissism.

Rumi gives helpful advice:

> Close your eyes, fall in love, stay there.[31]

LOVING HUMANKIND

The Quran never says that Allah is the God of *Muslims only* or *Arabs only*. Instead, the Quran teaches a prayer: **"Say: I seek refuge in the Lord of *humankind*, the King of *humankind*, the God of *humankind*"** (114:1– 3). In the verse above, Allah uses the word *humankind* three times to emphasize that He is the God of all humans. People who have love and devotion towards Allah tend to show compassion and kindness towards all His creations. The following quote by author Mahmoud Mostafa highlights the idea that true love for Allah naturally extends to compassion and love for all of humanity: "The relationship of love between us and Allah, between us and others, and between us and all of creation is essential to reaching our full potential as human beings. When we nourish our hearts with love, when we manifest Allah's love in our lives, with our families, with our friends, in our work, in our prayers, in everything that we do, the entire meaning of life changes for us, and our own experience of our humanness is transformed."[32]

The love we feel should be expressed through acts of kindness and charity: **"Spend [your] wealth out of *love for Him* [Allah] on relatives, orphans, the helpless, needy travelers, those who ask for money, and on the redemption of captives"** (2:177). The verse makes no distinctions based on age, tribe, race, religion, nationality, or sex. Also, the verse prioritizes charity recipients, with the believer's family at the top of the list. In other words, charity should begin at home and continue beyond.

It is worth mentioning that the instructions are generous, realistic, and logical. This verse also describes a beautiful motive for carrying out acts of charity: give *charity for the love of Allah.*

I AM UGLY, SO I DO NOT DESERVE LOVE

In conditional love, a person's physical appearance plays a significant role. That is why, when searching for a spouse, we look for a beautiful person because *it is easier to love a beautiful person.* The reason everyone loves babies is because babies are cute. As people age, they often lose their youthful appearance, which can affect their popularity.

What if one believes that I do not look good and concludes that Allah does not love me or that I do not deserve love? Or one thinks that Allah made me ugly, which means that Allah does not love me. For this line of thinking, the Quran has an important message. Allah made us the way we are at this moment, and *we are always beautiful to Allah.* The Quran says, **"He [Allah]** has given you shape and *made your shapes beautiful*" (40:64). In this verse, Allah assures us that at any age and under any circumstances, we are beautiful. Simply put, *we are good the way we are*. If omniscient Allah judges us as beautiful, there is no reason for us to have low self-esteem or withhold love from ourselves.

We all encounter various challenges in life, which are tests from Allah. Our parents, appearance, race, nationality, gender, and physical attributes are also tests from Allah. How we see ourselves, whether ugly or beautiful, depends entirely on our perception. However, it is essential to remember that Allah is our creator. According to verse (40:64), we are always beautiful in Allah's judgment, regardless of age or circumstances.

Sufi Malik Muhammad Jaisi (died- 1542 CE) was blind in one eye. Once, when he was passing through a village, some people made fun of his blind eye. Jaisy asked them, "Who are you laughing at, me or my Creator?" This question left the onlookers speechless.

Next time you see yourself in the mirror, tell yourself, "My Creator loves me the way I am right now." *Try it*. This statement is inspired by: **"He [Allah] is the All-forgiving, the Most Loving One"** (85:14) and the above verse (40:64).

The Prophet[PBUH] said, "Verily, Allah does not look at your appearance or wealth, but rather He looks at your hearts and actions."[33] We have a habit of giving too much importance to our looks. But unconditional love knows our true worth, which is far more precious than our physical appearance.

Rumi has some guidance to offer:

Achieve some perfection yourself so that you may not fall into sorrow by seeing the perfection in others.[34]

THE ISLAMIC ART OF HANDLING HEARTBREAK

Our emotional well-being critically depends on love. We spend our lives striving to love others and be loved by those dear to us. However, we are ultimately destined to be separated from them. Why? There can be several reasons, such as loss of interest, relocating due to a job or business, disagreements, cruelty, rejection, exploitation, abuse, conflicting interests, migration, and, inevitably, death.

When one understands that Allah is the only one who can make events happen and every hardship is a test from the benevolent and merciful Allah with a beneficial long-term goal, it becomes possible to emotionally accept whatever the compassionate Allah sends one's way. Emotionally, surrendering to Allah involves acknowledging that He is the ultimate planner and administrator of all events. We submit our hopes, plans, and outcomes to God's control and wisdom. Such a person does not blame anyone for personal difficulties.

Just a few days before his death, the Prophet[PBUH] received an emotional shock that his only surviving son, Ibrahim, was fatally sick. The infant died in his mother's lap as Prophet Muhammad[PBUH] was watching and crying. In this moment of extreme grief, he prayed, "The eyes send their tears, and the heart is saddened, but we do not say anything except that which please our Lord. O Ibrahim, we are grieving your departure."[35] This incident tells us that involuntary reactions to sad news, including expressing emotions and crying, are permitted in Islam. Even if Prophet Muhammad[PBUH] was deeply saddened, he emotionally accepted the decree of Allah. The Prophet[PBUH] did not blame anyone. Without blaming anyone, the scars of a broken heart tend to heal faster. Even in our saddest moments, the continuous flow of *unconditional love* of Allah from our hearts will constantly support us and keep us from breaking down.

All human love relationships eventually end in separation, but the continuous bond of unconditional love with Allah remains intact. We never lose by loving Allah the most. As a result, the loss of second-priority human love relationships will no longer feel like the end of the world. We feel Allah's love right in our hearts. Loving Him is necessary for us to find continuous peace and tranquility. It is an essential part of Islamic worship. Muslim theologian Ibn-Taymiyyah said:

> Even if it [the heart] attains all that it can enjoy of created things, it will not feel at peace or find tranquility because it has an inherent need for its Lord, for He is the focus of its worship, love, and seeking and this is the only way to attain joy, happiness, pleasure, peace, and tranquility.[36]

RAISING CHILDREN WITH LOVE AND MERCY

Believers are advised to bring up their children with unconditional love, mercy, and compassion. Once, the Prophet[PBUH] was playing and kissing his grandson Al-Hasan ibn Ali while talking to Aqr'a ibn Habis, who commented, "I have ten children and have never kissed any of them." This is centuries-old behavior where some dads perceive it as a sign of toughness not to openly express affection toward their kids. The Prophet[PBUH] replied succinctly, "He who does not show mercy to others will not be shown mercy."[37] Implying that Allah will not have mercy on such people on the Day of Judgment. In a few words, the Prophet[PBUH] conveyed thoughtful reality: *compassion, mercy, and love are not weaknesses; they are strengths.* These qualities connect us to humanity.

Another significant point is that the Prophet's[PBUH] statement applies to *all humans in all situations.* Those who seek mercy from Allah on the Day of Judgement must show mercy to others, especially to the vulnerable, including children.

ISLAM-INSPIRED LOVE AND MARRIAGE

Islam assigns different responsibilities to men and women. It is primarily the husband's responsibility to ensure that the family is well taken care of and to provide all reasonable assistance to the wife and family members. However, based on circumstances or personal preferences, the wife can also act as a provider to share or take over household responsibilities.

Suppose there is an argument between husband and wife, and the issue is not settled before bedtime. The author recommends that the husband should try to make peace, even if the wife is 100 percent wrong. *Yes, even then*! The husband does not have to agree to do what the wife wants; still, he should try to make up. *Who said that in family arguments, you must first unanimously prove who is guilty, and only then can you make peace?* This condition uselessly delays the peace process.

Most of the time, in family arguments, peace can be made without having to settle an issue. That is how children resolve disputes. They do not over-analyze until one party is unanimously proven guilty. The husband should take the initiative by expressing unconditional love for his wife in a way that she knows. Say, by lovingly caressing her. *Just try it!* Here, through affectionate gestures, the husband conveys to his wife that "Even if we have disagreements, my love for you is unconditional." If that happens, the wife should reciprocate with unconditional love. Prophet Muhammad[PBUH] said, "Each one of you is a shepherd and is responsible for those under his care."[38] You would be surprised at the power of unconditional love. Most arguments would end right there.

Even during arguments, unconditional love should always be in one's heart. Even if a woman is physically weaker, financially dependent, and has less education, she still has every right to express herself and disagree with her husband.

The above strategy is not suitable for *all* marital arguments. Sometimes, it is necessary to logically analyze and identify the problem before seeking a solution. For example, there are some concerns that neither husband nor wife should ignore, such as incidents of promiscuity, the welfare of children, and health.

Both husband and wife are responsible for guiding the family toward Islamic monotheism. If adult children do not believe in Islamic monotheism, gently but persistently explain without severing ties.

SUMMARY: LOVING ALLAH UNCONDITIONALLY

The highest level of satisfaction and contentment over a prolonged period is possible only when a believer unconditionally loves Allah the most and simultaneously feels Allah's love. This is inherently a spiritually gratifying and truly pleasant process that drastically reduces all kinds of suffering. It is like an infant who stops crying the moment her mother picks her up. The baby knows without a doubt that her mother loves her, and motivated by love, the baby trusts that her mother will remove every type of discomfort. Love brings instant satisfaction and contentment to the baby. And Allah is more loving and more merciful than all mothers in the world.

Loving Allah unconditionally and feeling His love is the only way to acquire the state of *Nafs-e-Mutma'inna,* or a "**(Fully) contented soul**" (89:27). Allah promises paradise to those who attain the state of *Nafs-e-Mutma'inna.* This goal is surprisingly realistic because Allah also knows our individual circumstances and limitations. All we have to do is aim our good intended efforts in the right direction and pray.

Rumi said,

> Make peace with the universe.
> Take joy in it.
> It will turn to gold.
> Resurrection will be now.
> Every moment, a new beauty.[39]

Let us all strive to love Allah

and

simultaneously feel His love.

"The strongest of the believers' love is their love of Allah" (2:165).

"He [Allah] is the All-forgiving, the Most Loving One" (85:14).

CHAPTER 2

ZULM: OPPRESSION AND INJUSTICE

The previous chapter explains that Islam requires spiritual growth through unconditional love and further explains that love is a feeling, not an action. What are the teachings of Islam regarding the *actions* or *behavior* of a Muslim towards oneself and others? Islam promotes the following two guidelines, leading to the same goal:

1. The Quran encourages *adl* (justice), along with its several synonyms, *insaf* (fairness) and *qist* (righteousness).[40]

2. The same idea is reinforced by repeatedly discouraging/prohibiting *zulm* (oppression and injustice). The Quran also prohibits various synonyms of zulm, including *baghy* (encroachment, abuse), *djawr* (oppression), *fisq* (moral deficiency), *inhiraf* (deviation), *mayl* (inclination), and *tughyan* (tyranny).[41]

According to Brill's Encyclopedia of Islam, the nearest translation of the Arabic word *zulm* would be *exceeding the appropriate limits of behavior in dealing with others while violating their essential human rights.*[42] Lane's Arabic-English dictionary defines zulm as *putting a thing in a place not its own.*[43] Any harmful/senseless action or concept is *zulm*. According to Abdul Mannan Omar's Dictionary of the Holy Quran, the word *zulm* encompasses the meanings of the English words oppression, tyranny, and injustice.[44]

To put it differently, if a person deprives others of their rights, it is zulm. At the same time, failing to fulfill duties and obligations towards others is also considered zulm.

It must be noted that the antonym of *zulm* is *adl*. By prohibiting *zulm* and simultaneously mandating *adl*, the Quran strongly prohibits all kinds of human rights violations.

One way to evaluate the emphasis of a concept in the Quran is to do a word count. The Quran greatly emphasizes justice by repeating the word adl 18 times (if the word adl is used in a different meaning, it is not counted here). The Quran conveys the *same* message by condemning oppression by using the word zulm an astounding 288 times (not counting occurrences of the same root word z-l-m, which means "Darkness").

Appendix A lists verse numbers in the Quran that use the words adl and zulm. Brill's Encyclopedia sums up the emphasis on *zulm* in the Quran: "It can be seen as one of the most important negative value-words in the sacred book.*"[45]*

EXAMPLES OF THE WORD *ZULM* USED IN THE QURAN

> **Those who misappropriate the property of orphans with *zulm* [unjustly] swallow but fire into their bellies (4:10).**
>
> **Allah does not love those who do *zulm* (3:57).**
>
> **Hellfire shall be their home, and evil is the home of those who do *zulm* (3:151).**

Zulm is man-made suffering inflicted on others. Allah says in hadith Nawawi [# 24], "O My servants, I have made oppression unlawful for Me and unlawful for you, so do not commit oppression against one another."[46] Allah does not do zulm on humans: **"God has not done injustice to them [humans], but they have wronged themselves"** (9:70).

Islamic Principle of 'Live and Let Live'

Here is the Islamic version of the 'golden rule' of social behavior: **"Do no zulm, and you will not be subjected to zulm"** (2:279). If people follow this rule, they will avoid unjust behavior and simplify their lives. The positive impact will extend to society, resulting in decreased conflict and fewer adverse outcomes.

SUBSET OF SITUATIONS WHERE ZULM IS PROHIBITED

Islam strictly prohibits zulm in *all human interactions and in all circumstances throughout life.* This section offers a few specific examples.

ZULM OF RACIAL PREJUDICE

Pagan Arabs used to look down upon blacks from neighboring Africa as an inferior race. Far ahead of his time, the Prophet[PBUH] permanently *prohibited racial prejudice in Islam.*

A companion, Abu Dhar, referred to a black enslaved person as the *son of a black woman.* This was considered an insult. When the Prophet[PBUH] heard the comment, he said to Abu Dhar, "Are you insulting this man with his mother? Truly, *you possess some of the qualities of the era of Ignorance (pre-Islamic times)."[47]* Later, Abu Dhar sincerely apologized to the enslaved man. The Prophet[PBUH] treated all people as equal, and he successfully changed the thinking of Muslims, even when the concept of racial equality was totally beyond the culture of his era. Compare this to racial prejudice practiced in many societies today.

ZULM AGAINST CHILDREN

Islam teaches parents to be fair to all children and not to mistreat or do zulm to less favored children. Once, a man planned to give a gift from his wealth to his favorite child while ignoring the rest of his children. He requested Prophet Muhammad[PBUH] to witness the gift. The Prophet[PBUH] asked: "Did you offer the same to all your children?" The man replied, "No!" Prophet refused to be the witness and said: "Fear Allah and be just in dealing with your children."[48]

Islam prohibited zulm against defenseless children more than 1400 years ago, but unfortunately, child abuse remains a problem to this day.

ZULM AGAINST PARENTS

Elderly parents are often sick, frail, and irritable. They lose their good looks and dispositions, and caring for them involves time and effort. This makes aged parents vulnerable, particularly when they are dependent on their independent adult children. The Quran protects elderly parents against physical, mental, and emotional abuse, ensuring their rights are safeguarded, **"You shall be kind to your parents; if one or both of them live to their old age in your lifetime, you shall not say to them any word of contempt nor repel them, and you shall address them in kind words"** (17:23). In all matters, **"Be kind to your parents"** (4:36).

The Quran preached this 1400 years ago. Compare this to modern-day practices, where many people place their elderly parents in nursing homes, even if they are not critically sick. Such a lack of moral values has caused a lot of pain and suffering for the elderly and is not in the spirit of the teachings of Islam.

RIGHTS OF THE DISABLED

When Muhammad[PBUH] was head of state in Medina, he sometimes had to leave the city. On such occasions, he would appoint someone to temporarily take charge of the affairs of the state. On several occasions, he gave this great responsibility to Abdullah ibn Umm Makhtoom.[49] This was a significant responsibility. Any decision he made would have affected everyone.

Brace yourself for a surprise. Abdullah Ibn Umme Makhtoom was blind. Can you imagine the recognition of the rights of people with disabilities 1400 years ago? Even today, in some parts of the world, people with disabilities are treated worse than animals.

The Prophet[PBUH] not only envisioned the rights of people with disabilities but gave them authority and responsibility about 1400 years ago.

ZULM OF VIOLATING THE PRIVACY OF AN INDIVIDUAL

Islam provides various measures to safeguard individuals' privacy and other rights. Here are just three examples:

1. **Do not spy on one another** (49:12).
2. **Refrain from speaking negatively or slandering one another.** (49:12).
3. **O believers! Do not enter houses other than your own until you have sought permission** (24:27).

ZULM ON THE DOWNTRODDEN

The Quran safeguards the rights of all the oppressed and underprivileged individuals: **"Feed the poor, the orphan and the prisoners *for the love of Allah*"** (76:8). This verse instructs Muslims to show their love for Allah through charity towards the vulnerable, irrespective of their religion or race. When Muslim General Khalid bin Waleed took over the Heerah in Iraq, where almost the entire population was non-Muslim, he declared the following laws, "Any elderly person, disabled worker, terminally ill person, or a rich person who went bankrupt and based on that deserves charity from the fellow religious people, will not be required to pay head-tax. Furthermore, each one will become entitled to suitable allowances from the Islamic Treasury for himself and his dependents."[50]

Khalid bin Waleed must have meticulously weighed all options to prevent any form of injustice.

ZULM OF WASTING NATURAL RESOURCES

Prophet Muhammad[PBUH] said, "Do not waste [water] even if performing ablution on the bank of a fast flowing large river."[51] The idea of preservation and avoiding wastage is not limited to water. All the natural resources we have are not a coincidence. They are the blessings of Allah and should be used to benefit humanity. This principle has never been more relevant than today. All types of destruction of natural resources, including deforestation, contamination, soil erosion, air pollution, fossil fuel consumption, and overfishing, are zulm. These actions cause significant harm to the environment and are inconsistent with Islamic teachings.

ZULM IN BUSINESS TRANSACTIONS

All business transactions should be fair and just. The Quran condemns those who cheat in business by measuring improperly. **"Woe to those who defraud, [when] they take by measure from men [others], take the full measure, but when they give by measure to others, they give less than due"** (83:1–3).

Fair dealing is not limited to selling merchandise. This verse states a general rule that in all business and social transactions, give and take should be fair and just. This means that individuals should not exploit others. Both parties should mutually agree on a reasonable price for goods and services. Furthermore, people should not exploit others' trust, vulnerability, or lack of knowledge.

ZULM ON EMPLOYEES AND ENSLAVED PEOPLE

One of the latest management strategies is to treat employees respectfully and avoid overburdening them. Prophet Muhammad[PBUH] gave the same message several centuries ago, "[Workers] are your brothers, and Allah has put them under your command. So, whoever has a brother under his command should feed him of what he himself eats and dress him of what he himself wears. Do not ask them to do things beyond their capacity, and if you do so, then help them."[52]

ZULM BY THE EMPLOYEES

It is also zulm if employees do not fulfill their assigned duties, whether out of carelessness or laziness. Prophet Muhammad[PBUH] said: "Whoever wants to earn an honest living is on my Sunnah [tradition] and does not harm people [commits no zulm] will be admitted to Paradise."[53]

ZULM ON ANIMALS

Islamic fair treatment also extends to protecting animals who are unable to voice their complaints. Owners are responsible for treating their pets humanely. Prophet Muhammad[PBUH] said, "A woman entered the (Hell) Fire because of a cat which she had tied, neither giving it food nor setting it free to eat from the pests of the Earth."[54]

In addition to physical abuse, the Prophet[PBUH] also forbade the mental abuse of animals. He instructed that if you plan to slaughter an animal to eat its meat, *do not sharpen the knife in front of the animal.* Also, before the slaughter, *to reduce the animal's suffering*, make sure the blade is sharp.[55]

Please compare it to many cultures, even today, where live animals are eaten while animals are conscious enough to feel the excruciating pain of dismemberment. For example, Octopus (Sannakji), Fish (Ikizukuri), Sea Urchin (Uni), Frog Sashimi, and Casu Marzu Cheese. In Spanish bullfighting, the animal endures several stages of torment, causing immense physical and psychological suffering.

ZULM, BY GIVING FALSE WITNESS

False testimony in a court of law can result in the punishment of an innocent. Islam strongly forbids the zulm from giving false evidence. **"O believers!** *Be steadfast for the sake of Allah* **and bear true witness and let not the enmity of a people incite you to do injustice;** *do justice***; that is nearer to piety. Fear Allah, surely Allah is fully aware of all your actions"** (5:8).

Furthermore, Islam requires that judges be fair and impartial and that justice be served regardless of personal ties, *even if the guilty person is a loved one* of the judge. The Quran says, **"O believers! Stand firm for justice and bear true witness for the sake of Allah, even though it be against yourselves, your parents, or your relatives. It does not matter whether the party is rich or poor – Allah is the well-wisher of both. So let not your selfish desires swerve you from justice. If you distort your**

testimony or decline to give it, then you should remember that Allah is fully aware of your actions" (4:135).

A rich or influential person is not above the law. It should be noted that both the above verses end with a stern warning from Allah.

EXAMPLE OF ISLAMIC UNBIASED JUSTICE

Islam regards justice as the birthright of all humans, regardless of their religion. The Quran has strict instructions for judges of every court: **"When you judge between people, judge with fairness"** (4:58).

Taima ibn Ubairaq was a Muslim who stole a bag of flour and armor from his neighbor and planted them in the house of a Jew. The theft was reported to Prophet Muhammad[PBUH], and eventually, the stolen items were recovered from the Jew's house. Taima ibn Ubairaq had strong tribal support. His fellow Muslim tribe members pressured Prophet Muhammad[PBUH] to pass a quick judgment against the Jew. However, before the judgment, Allah revealed to Prophet Muhammad[PBUH] that the Jew was innocent and indicted Taima ibn Ubairaq. In this context, the following verse was revealed: **"Judge between people in accordance with the Right Way which Allah has shown you, so be not an advocate for those who betray trust"** (4:105)[56]. It is the duty of a Muslim judge to ensure impartial justice, regardless of social pressure, religion, or race of the parties involved.

THE END RESULT OF ALL LEGAL JUDGMENTS MUST AVOID ZULM

What if a judge passes a legal decision based on a Quranic rule, but the circumstances indicate that *obeying the rule would result in zulm*? In that case, *the rule would change* because avoiding zulm is a higher priority. It is the prominently emphasized principle of the Quran.

Here is an example. During the lifetime of Prophet Muhammad[PBUH,] two men fought, and one of them bit the hand of the other person. In response, the person pulled his hand away, and the biter lost a tooth. The Quran allows for equal punishment for damages - a tooth for a tooth - unless the victim chooses to forgive (5:45). In this incident, the person who lost the tooth insisted on punishment and took the case to Prophet Muhammad[PBUH]. The Prophet[PBUH] refused to punish the person who pulled his hand away and asked the plaintiff, "Should he leave his hand in your mouth so that you might snap it ...[sic] like a camel?"[57]

In general, this is an important principle that can be applied not only to court proceedings but also to everyday life. Muslims should consider the *consequences* of all their actions, even while obeying the laws of Islamic Jurisprudence[58].

NO ONE IS ABOVE THE LAW

When the Prophet[PBUH] was the ruler of Medina and surrounding areas. At that time, he was the top religious leader of the Muslims and head of the Legislative, Judiciary, and Executive. "A man came to the Prophet[PBUH] demanding his debts and behaved rudely. The companions of the Prophet[PBUH] intended to harm him, but the Prophet[PBUH] said, "Leave him, for the creditor has the right to speak…Give him a camel of the same age as his camel [that was much more valuable than the original loan]."[59] This incident illustrates that the Prophet [PBUH] allowed freedom of speech to the man. Moreover, on legal grounds, every citizen had the right to challenge anyone, including the head of the state. *Islam teaches that no one is above the law.*

NOT GUILTY BY ASSOCIATION

In 631 CE, a Christian delegation from the city of Najran visited Muhammad[PBUH] for religious debate. Pragmatically, this certainly was not the best occasion for a visit by a Christian delegation. By this time, the Muslims had taken over Mecca, and Muhammad[PBUH] was fully recognized as the head of state.

Just two years earlier, the Christian ruler Heraclius of the Eastern Roman Empire demonstrated open hostility toward the growing Islamic power, which resulted in the Battle of Mu'tah between Christians and Muslims. In 630, Muhammad[PBUH] heard reports that Heraclius planned to attack Muslims in Medina. Consequently, the Prophet[PBUH] had to prepare the army to confront the Romans (described in chapter 3 of this book). At the time of the delegation's visit, the Christian Roman Empire was a clear threat to Muslims.

Despite the possibility of an assassination attempt by the Christians from Najran, Muhammad[PBUH] warmly welcomed the delegation with traditional Arab hospitality. He received them in the famous Al-Masjid an-Nabawi, regarded as the second holiest mosque in Islam. They had a friendly debate. After the debate, Muhammad[PBUH] signed a treaty with the Christians for peaceful coexistence and gave them the freedom to practice their religion in Najran. The treaty stated that "to the Christians of Najran and neighboring treaties, the security of Allah and pledge of His Prophet are extended for their lives, their religion, their property – to those present as well as those absent and other besides."[60] Later, the Christian delegation returned to Najran in peace.

A paranoid king would have thought that *all* Christians were a threat and assumed that the visitors had some sinister motive. Therefore, the visitors should be punished. Kings usually try to increase their influence by humiliating and trampling the weak and unprotected. Instead, the Prophet[PBUH] did not make any false assumption that all Christians are enemies. Modern civilization generally recognizes that crimes committed by a few community members do not mean the entire community is criminal. Imagine the wisdom and foresight of the Prophet[PBUH] when he decided that association alone does not provide sufficient evidence to convict someone of a crime. He believed in thoroughly examining all available evidence and testimony to determine guilt. Otherwise, it would be *injustice and zulm.*

FORGIVENESS FOR THOSE WHO DO ZULM

During the initial stage of his prophethood, the Prophet preached Islam in Mecca. He was exceptionally dedicated and sincere, and his sermons were highly effective. People from all walks of life began to convert to Islam. However, the introduction of Islam as a new religion posed a challenge to the traditional pagan beliefs of Mecca, which were followed by the overwhelming majority of its citizens. Additionally, they viewed Islam as a threat to their social, family, and economic frameworks.

To contain Islam, the pagans relentlessly oppressed the converts and the Prophet[PBUH]. Imagine the pressure on the Prophet[PBUH], who was trying to protect the new Muslims, while he himself was a target of insults, ridicule, and physical attacks. A pagan leader once hit the Prophet[PBUH] so hard that his head bled.

Muslims who were poor or enslaved and without tribal protection suffered the most. Enslaved Yasir and his wife, Sumayya, suffered terrible torture. They were repeatedly forced to lie on the burning hot sand and severely beaten. Their Muslim son Ammar was at times tossed up on burning coals. Eventually, Yasir and Sumayya died, but they refused to renounce Islam.[61] Another enslaved person, Bilal bin Rabah, was mercilessly tortured:

"Sometimes a rope was put around his neck, and street boys were made to drag him through the streets and even across the hillocks of Makkah. At times, he was subjected to prolonged deprivation of food and drink; at others, he was bound up, made to lie down on the burning sand and under the crushing burden of heavy stones."[62] Still, Bilal refused to recant Islam. An enslaved woman, "Zinnira was beaten so harshly that she lost her eyesight."[63] Other enslaved women, Lubaina, Nadia, and Umm Umais, were mercilessly tortured. Enslaved Khabbab bin Al-Aratt "Experienced exemplary torture and maltreatment. The Makkan polytheists used to pull his hair and twist his neck and made him lie on burning coal with a big rock on his chest to prevent him from escaping."[64] None of them renounced Islam. Many victims of torture requested the Prophet[PBUH] to find a way to end the ongoing oppression. At that time, the Prophet[PBUH] could only preach to Muslims to be patient and pray to Allah. Throughout this time, he was unable to provide a practical solution for all Muslims in Mecca.

To further harass the Muslims, the pagans forced the Prophet[PBUH] and his followers to leave Mecca and live in an unpopulated area for almost three years, pushing them to the brink of starvation. The hardship was so severe that, shortly after the period of expulsion, the Prophet's Uncle Abu Talib and his wife, Khadijah, died.

After several years of relentless efforts to protect Muslims, finally, the Prophet[PBUH] managed to find a safe home for Muslims in the nearby city of Medina. Then he ordered Muslims in Mecca to migrate there, and towards the very end, the Prophet[PBUH] himself migrated. Even after the migration, pagan armies attacked Muslims in Medina on several occasions. Many Muslims were killed in those attacks.

The Prophet[PBUH] preferred to forgive a *zalim* [person who commits zulm] instead of punishing them. One excellent example of this occurred during the conquest of Mecca, when tables turned, and the Prophet[PBUH] became the ruler of Mecca (with the least amount of violence). He generously forgave almost *the entire* pagan population, even after they had ridiculed, humiliated, oppressed, tortured, and killed many Muslims, including many close family members of the Prophet[PBUH]. Realistically speaking, can you imagine anyone else being so generous? Please do not forget that these are historical events, not mythology.

ZULM ON THE POWS

Across the globe, armies have been torturing prisoners of war since the dawn of humankind to the present day. Only relatively recently have POW rights been codified in the Geneva Conventions of 1949 and 1929. However, implementing those laws is altogether a different story. What was the Prophet's[PBUH] attitude towards POWs 1400 years ago?

After Muslims migrated to the city of Medina, Mecca's pagans attacked them on several occasions. The first major pagan attack resulted in the Battle of Badr. Muslims won the battle and captured many pagan prisoners. The Prophet[PBUH] not only instructed his army to treat prisoners of war humanely but also ensured their rights were protected in practice.

Muslims gave the POWs bread to eat while they themselves ate only dates, which was considered a far inferior food. The Prophet[PBUH] permitted all traditionally accepted means to free POWs expeditiously. For example, the Prophet[PBUH] allowed the existing Arab tradition of freeing a POW if someone paid a fine on his behalf.

These POWs were not only soldiers of an aggressive army, but some were directly responsible for oppressing and torturing Muslims. One prominent pagan public speaker, Suhail ibn Amar, was among these POWs. He used his oratory skills to instigate the attack against Muslims. In that era, Arab poets and public orators used to sway the decision of the crowd and sometimes even the rulers to go to war. A prominent companion of the Prophet who later became the second guided Caliph, Umar asked Prophet's[PBUH] permission to remove Suhail ibn Amar's front teeth so he would never again use his oratory skills against Muslims. The Prophet[PBUH] said: "Were I to do this, Allah would disfigure me on the Day of Judgment, despite the fact that I am His messenger."[65] It is important to note that even though the Prophet[PBUH] was the most prominent religious leader of Muslims, he remained humble and down-to-earth. According to Islamic teachings, on the Day of Judgment, Allah will judge every human being, including the prophets.

In contrast, some religious leaders claim to have a god-given right to harm, torture, or kill individuals. For example, at the ancient Maya site of Chichén Itzá, human sacrifices were carried out to please the rain god. Such reckless behavior shows a complete disregard for the lives of fellow human beings.[66]

In contrast, the Prophet[PBUH] prohibited all forms of torture against non-Muslim POWs from an attacking army and expressed concern about facing Allah's judgment. Such a person can never do zulm on others. It is quite remarkable how different these two approaches were!

The humane treatment of POWs in the Battle of Badr was not an isolated incident. After defeating pagans in the Battle of Hunayn, the Prophet[PBUH] let POWs go free.[67]

The sad reality is that our modern world has discovered many kinds of methods of torture, including electric shock and waterboarding. In striking contrast, 1400 years ago, the Prophet[PBUH] practiced *humane* treatment of POWs. He said that if a mother and daughter are captured as POWs, do not separate them, and non-Muslim POWs were never forced to convert to Islam. Prophet Muhammad[PBUH] also exchanged non-Muslim POWs for Muslim POWs.[68]

MISCELLANEOUS TYPES OF ZULM

Compassion and empathy are an indispensable part of Islam. Here are some examples:

Believers must be sensitive to the feelings of fellow human beings and respect their privacy. Believers are instructed to give gifts to one another and accept gifts from others; they are not allowed to read other people's letters secretly and must always be polite to everyone. After performing acts of kindness, believers are advised against boasting about them or making the recipients uncomfortable by reminding them of the favors. If someone asks for some favor or alms, then a believer has only two options: either help the needy or *politely* refuse. However, believers cannot humiliate the needy person or use sarcasm.

THE WORST ZULM OF ALL

The Quran *precisely* defines: **"Surely committing *polytheism is the worst zulm*"** (31:13). Allah alone is our Creator and Sustainer. Suppose a person worships any other imaginary god or human or any other part of creation instead of Allah or along with Allah; that person commits the sin of polytheism. In that case, as suggested by verse 31:13 above, it is the most significant form of zulm or misguided belief. Why? Because zulm is defined as *putting a thing in a place that is not its own*. Allocating divinity to a part of creation or an imaginary entity is the most critical misplacement error. A polytheist can only be saved by repenting to Allah and believing in Islamic monotheism during their earthly life.

KEEPING RELIGIOUS RITUALS EASY AND PRACTICAL

Three companions of the prophet decided to make the Islamic rituals more challenging. One person decided that he would not sleep; another one said that he would never break the fast (and die in the state of fasting); and the last one stated that he would never marry. When the Prophet[PBUH] heard their decisions, he said, "I fast and end my fast (at sunset, when Muslims are expected to end the fast), I sleep, and I marry women. So, he who does not follow my religious traditions is not from me (not one of my followers)." [69] In other words, if a person alters the Islamic rituals by *adding* zulm, then that person does not remain a Muslim.

This hadith has another message: In all circumstances, believers should *avoid doing voluntarily zulm on themselves*. Muslims should be kind to themselves and treat themselves with fairness and dignity. It emphasizes the importance of practicing *self-care and self-love*. The Quran says, "**God does not love the unjust**" (3:57).

ISLAM STANDS OUT: NO SELF-INFLICTED EMOTIONAL ZULM

What about psychological zulm on one's own self? What if, instead of striving to be peaceful and content, an individual allows negative emotions like anger, depression, guilt, or fear to persist? This kind of emotional zulm-on-self is not permitted. To have a "**(Fully) contented soul**" (89:27), A Muslim should constantly attempt to attain tranquility, peace, and contentment. Such positive emotions are the consequences if one has unconditional love towards Allah, self, and others.

The problem is that life's ups and downs present all kinds of challenges to our inner peace. The good news is that Islam teaches us how to achieve the incredible goal of having a fully satisfied soul (details will be discussed later in this book). For example, Prophet Muhammad[PBUH] taught a prayer for inner peace: "O Allah! I seek refuge in You from worry and grief, from incapacity and laziness, from cowardice and miserliness, from being heavily in debt, and from being overpowered by (other) men." [70]

Islam provides solutions to several emotional problems. Only one instance is described here:

CONTROLLING THE ANGER

Allah says: **"When they [the righteous Muslims] are angry, they forgive"** (42:37). This verse not only points out the issue of anger, but it provides the solution: *forgiveness*. If left unaddressed, anger can haunt our minds for decades, persisting long after an upsetting event has ended. It can lead to feelings of resentment, bitterness, and even depression. This means we must try our best to forgive. At times, it may involve personal sacrifice and difficult adjustment. But, usually, forgiving and forgetting leads to healthier relationships.

AMAZING SOLUTION: ISLAM ALLOWS VERY REALISTIC EXCEPTION

What if someone hurts you so deeply that you never want to associate with that offender or see them again? The emotional wounds may be too severe to heal. There can be another valid reason: what if the offender repeats the same offense?

These situations cause a conflict: (1) Islam insists on forgiveness, but (2) in some cases, if a victim makes up with the offender, the victim would be doing *zulm-on-self* (as in the two cases described in the previous paragraph). All forms of zulm-on-self are also prohibited in Islam. In such situations, *how does one forgive without doing zulm-on-self?* How can we solve this seemingly impossible paradox?

The beauty of Islam is that it offers a *practical solution* to this paradox. As the Quran suggests, you forgive the offender in your heart. But if you are uncomfortable or emotionally not ready, you do not have to associate or socialize with the offender, as that would cause zulm on yourself.

We all have human limitations. At times, we are simply unable to associate with the offender. In the Battle of Uhud, the pagan Wahshi ibn Harb killed Hamza, who was a Muslim and the Prophet's uncle. Later, Wahshi ibn Harb converted to Islam. The Prophet[PBUH] welcomed him into Islam, *forgave him, and did not punish* him for the heinous murder. However, the Prophet[PBUH] said he did not wish to see Wahshi ibn Harb's face. In other words, the Prophet instructed Wahshi ibn Harb not to appear within his sight.

Therefore, the solution is to forgive in your heart, but if you are uncomfortable, *you have the right to keep the offender out of your life.* If you choose not to associate with the offender, depending on the situation, you may decide not to inform the offender that you have forgiven. Such a decision not only protects you but also sets an example for the offender. It can discourage the offender from engaging in similar behavior in the future. If the situation requires it, taking legal action is also feasible. The bottom line is Allah does not want you to suffer or do zulm on yourself.

If you follow the Quran's advice, handling your anger becomes a win-win situation. In both of the following options, you will be protecting yourself from zulm:

(1) you forgive the offender in your heart. Islam regards forgiveness as a good deed. Your anger will fade away.
(2) You still have the freedom to decide if you want to socially make up with the offender.

What a beautiful yet practical solution!

ZULM OF SELF-DESTRUCTIVE HABITS

Self-destructive habits like substance abuse, gambling, and playing the lottery are prohibited in Islam. **"O believers! Intoxicants and gambling ... and division by arrows (lottery) are the filthy works of Satan"** (5:90).

ZULM OF SELF-IMPOSED FINANCIAL HARDSHIP

Islam strongly advocates charity. A form of charity, *zakat*, is one of the five pillars of Islam. But what if a person donates all their worldly possessions and becomes bankrupt? That would be a financial disaster for donors and their families. In addition, this could cause emotional suffering in the form of self-pity and regret. *Both self-imposed emotional and financial sufferings are prohibited.* Likewise, if a person wastes excess wealth on unnecessary luxuries, that would also be zulm. Allah praises **"Those who, when they spend, are not extravagant and not niggardly, but hold a just balance between those (extremes)"** (25:67). This verse also suggests that if you have wealth, you should use it for your essential personal needs and not be overly stingy.

PROTECTING YOURSELF FROM THE OPPRESSION OF OTHERS

When Muslims have a choice, they are *required to avoid* becoming victims of zulm. Allah praises those who **"Defend themselves when wronged"** (26:227).How do you defend yourself from the zulm of others? Islam provides strict guidelines. The first step is to exhaust all *nonviolent* options to protect yourself from zulm. One excellent example of this comes from the Treaty of Hudaybia. With profound insight, Prophet Muhammad[PBUH] saved Muslims from an all-out battle that would have caused heavy fatalities on both sides (described in Chapter 4 of this book).

Depending on the circumstances, another option is to forgive the offender. And the last resort is for Muslims to use violence in self-defense. *However, Muslims are not allowed to exceed the original oppression caused by an offender.* To put it differently, *keep the defensive-aggression within reasonable limits.* The Quran says, **"Fight in the way of Allah with those who fight with you [attack you] and do not exceed the limits; surely Allah does not love those who exceed the limits"** (2:190). That is because excessive aggression under the guise of defensive measures can lead to zulm on the *offender.*

What if a person is completely helpless and unable to protect themselves from zulm? Islam regards such a person as a victim who is neither responsible for zulm-on-self nor a sinner. Victims of oppression should continue striving to protect themselves, remain hopeful and patient, and pray to Allah for relief. Allah promises forgiveness to helpless victims.

For example, Islam strictly prohibits prostitution. However, back then, some non-Muslims used to force their enslaved girls into prostitution. The Quran talks about the victims: **"If anyone forces girls into prostitution, then surely after such a *compulsion* Allah will be forgiving and be merciful to the girls"** (24:33).

A GLIMPSE OF ISLAMIC JUSTICE: COMPENSATION FOR ZULM ON OTHERS

Suppose an offender illegally acquires someone else's land. For such an offender, seeking forgiveness *only* from Allah is not enough. The initial step is to return the land to the victim and fully compensate the victim for all damages. Only after that does the offender become eligible to seek forgiveness from Allah.

The sinner must acknowledge the mistake and feel remorse. Taking full responsibility for one's sins is mandatory in Islam, so the offender avoids repeating the sin. To repent, the believer should say *Astaghfirullah* (I seek forgiveness from Allah). Say it with humility and genuine intention to avoid repeating the sin. Also, try to avoid all other sins. One should try to learn from the mistake and use it as an opportunity to become a better person. After that, if Allah wills, He may forgive the wrongdoer.

However, one should not use the guilt of past sins as an excuse to distance oneself from Allah. In hopelessness, a person may even quit worshipping Allah. Remember that **"He [Allah] is the <u>All-forgiving</u>, the Most Loving One"** (85:14).

An alternative to giving compensation is to seek forgiveness from the *victim*. The victim is given a choice to take equal (but not more) revenge or to forgive the offender. From the victim's point of view, forgiving the offender is highly recommended. Allah may also forgive the offender (based on the offense) and may reward the victim. Otherwise, on the Day of Judgment, the offender would be *fully* responsible for the zulm on a fellow human being. No oppression or injustice is too small. **"Whoever has done an atom's weight of evil shall see it"** (99:7–8). This shows the beauty of Islamic justice, in which the *victim of zulm is fully compensated unless the victim chooses to forgive.*

WHEN ISLAM CHANGES ITS OWN RULES?

Allah does not mandate any worship ritual that is extremely difficult or impossible to perform. Why? The answer is obvious – to avoid zulm. For example, Islam does not expect a Muslim priest to observe lifelong sexual abstinence. Instead, all Muslims are encouraged to get married. Similarly, Muslims are not required to shun the world. They are encouraged to fully engage in daily life, provided they avoid zulm/sins.

Ritual fasting from dawn to dusk is so important that it is considered one of the five pillars of Islam. Breaking the fast before dusk is a sin. But suppose while fasting, a person becomes too sick to continue and has to break the fast to avoid a health crisis. Does that make the person a sinner? No. Fasting and other worship rituals are essential, but only if they do not cause undue hardship. **"Allah never wishes injustice to his creation"** (40:31). Here, we see that Islam changes its own rules, according to the circumstances, to avoid zulm.

Those who are too old or sick to fast do not have to. They have the option to donate to charity or make up a missed fast. No person is responsible for anything beyond their capability.

Similarly, Islam provides alternatives for those who are too sick to perform the physical movements of obligatory ritual supplication or *salah*. In the context of the Hajj pilgrimage, Islam provides options for those who lack the financial or physical ability to travel.

AVOID ZULM EVEN WHILE DOING GOOD DEEDS

The above section shows that if, under certain circumstances, following a rule of Allah may *lead* to zulm, then Allah changes His own rules and worship rituals to protect humankind from zulm.

This shows a general Islamic principle. *If, under certain situations, a good intended action is likely to lead to zulm, then under those circumstances, Islam prohibits that particular action.* This principle created a subject called *Maqasid al-Sharia*. For centuries, Muslim scholars have been studying *Maqasid al-Sharia*.

Here is one example. Digging a well is a good deed because it provides water for travelers. However, digging a well in the middle of the road would become a safety hazard; therefore, it is no longer a good deed.

FREEDOM OF SPEECH AGAINST ZULM

Islam firmly commands: **"Do not slander one another"** (49:12). Is the *victim* of zulm allowed to speak against the offender? The Quran responds to this question with a clear *yes*: **"Allah does not like evil words to be uttered *except* by someone who is truly wronged"** (4:148). This amazing verse allows people to speak up against offenders, even if they are religious leaders or belong to the ruling class.

Once, Caliph Umar announced a newly created law in the mosque, which placed an upper limit on the amount of dowry to be paid by a man to his prospective bride. Right in the middle of his speech, an elderly woman spoke: "Allah gave the right to women, then, Umar, how dare you place such restriction?" Then she quoted verse 4:20. At that point, Caliph Umar publicly announced, "Umar is wrong, and the woman is right!" and immediately withdrew the proposed law. At that time, the caliph was not only head of state but also head of the Muslim clergy and judiciary.

Nonetheless, based on the correct reasoning, an ordinary old woman had the right to reject the caliph's opinion.[71] *In Islam, what is being said is more valuable and important than the status of the person saying it.* When evaluating a proposed idea, listeners should focus on the content, not the speaker's social or political status. Once again, nobody is above the law.

It is noteworthy that the woman opposed Caliph Umar with a *logical argument and proof from the Quran.* Islam does not allow illogical and humiliating verbal attacks, which is considered just another form of zulm. Equal credit goes to Caliph Umar, who not only withdrew the proposed law but *publicly* admitted his mistake. Only a great person can do that.

The above verse 4:148 also proves that a human did not author the Quran. If a human had authored the Quran, that person would have expected blind obedience from all followers, regardless of whether the command was fair or unfair. Instead, Allah has given individuals full freedom of speech, allowing the oppressed to seek justice for their grievances regardless of the oppressor's religious, political, or social status.

ISLAM RESTRICTS THE MISUSE OF POWER (ZULM) BY RELIGIOUS LEADERS

There are many instances in history when the priestly class of some religions claimed to control the divine and life after death. The priestly class has also claimed that they have the authority to forgive sins and bless whom they choose. They have, at times, controlled the masses and even the ruling class. This power has often given religious leaders the unmitigated authority to do financial, political, and social zulm. For example, about 500 years ago, in one temple dedicated to appease the gods, the South American Aztecs performed the human sacrifices of an estimated 80,000 people.[72]

Amazingly, Islam imposed restrictions on the authority of religious leaders to protect future Muslim generations from zulm. According to Islam, on the Day of Judgment, Allah *alone* will judge every human being, *including the prophets.* Only Allah can forgive.

As in the case of the woman who objected to Umar's law, Islam authorizes the Muslim masses to question religious leaders and protect themselves from zulm. Further, Islam does not define any religious hierarchy of the priest class. In a mosque, any qualified man can lead congregational prayers. In summary, Islam limits the authority of the scholars or Imams (prayer leaders) primarily to preaching. Besides praying to Allah, they have no power to intervene in divine affairs.

COMPASSION EVEN FOR THE ZALIM

With so much emphasis on avoiding zulm in all aspects of life, how should a Muslim treat a zalim? A Muslim should try to guide the zalim to give up zulm. Prophet Muhammad[PBUH] said: "Help your brother, whether he is an oppressor or an oppressed one." People asked, "O Allah's Apostle! It is all right to help him if he is oppressed, but how should we help him if he is an oppressor?" The prophet said, "By preventing him from oppressing others."[73] What a profound statement!

We have seen many examples above where Islam guides believers to refrain from committing zulm on others and themselves. The Prophet's[PBUH] above statement tries to protect a zalim, *even in life after death*, by trying to prevent the offender from committing zulm. This is yet another example of Islamic pure, unconditional love.

THE SUPPORTERS OF A ZALIM ARE ALSO SINNERS

The Quran mandates: **"Do not be inclined to those who are *unjust,* lest you be seized by the fire [of hell]"** (11:113). This verse is a universal rule applicable to all social and political situations. Without the help of supporters and collaborators, no leader/ruler can do zulm on the general population. Suppose a zalim leader plans to do zulm on a large group; then, the leader should not be able to find Muslim supporters because anyone who supports a zalim leader will also face punishment from Allah. As a result, the leader's plan to do large-scale zulm should fail. What a beautiful, far-reaching insight! It serves as a reminder to look beyond the obvious and consider the broader perspective.

ISLAM PROHIBITS ZULM ON PEACEFUL NON-MUSLIMS

The Quran clearly explains whom Muslims are allowed to fight: **"God does not forbid you to deal kindly and justly with those who have not fought against you about the religion or expelled you from your homes. God does not love the unjust people"** (60:8). In other words, fight only in self-defense or to claim what was forcefully taken away from you.

Treating all humans, including non-Muslims, with kindness is a universal rule of Islam. A female companion of the Prophet[PBUH] asked, "My mother is visiting me … shall I keep good relations with her?" The Prophet[PBUH] said, "Yes, keep good relations with her."[74] Just because someone does not follow Islam is not a justification to mistreat them.

Here is another example. Once, the Prophet[PBUH] and a few companions were sitting near a road, and a funeral procession passed by. In response, the Prophet[PBUH] stood up till the procession passed. To imitate the Prophet[PBUH], companions also stood up with him. Later, the Prophet[PBUH] was told that the deceased was a Jew. The Prophet[PBUH] gave a thought-provoking response, "Was he not a human being, or did he not have a soul?"[75] Showing respect to all humans is essential.

Even when Muslims have the upper hand, they are instructed to commit no zulm to non-Muslims under any pretext. The Prophet[PBUH] said, "Beware, if anyone wrongs [does zulm to] a *mu`ahid* [ a non-Muslim enjoying the protection of Muslims], or diminishes his right, or forces him to work beyond his capacity, or takes from him anything without his consent, I shall be his adversary on the Day of Judgment."[76] This means that if a Muslim does zulm on a *mu`ahid,* then s/he will be fully accountable on the Day of Judgment.

Based on the Quran and hadith, author Louay Fatoohi conclusively proved in his book *Jihad in the Quran* that a peaceful non-Muslim is not an enemy.[77]

SUPPRESSING RELIGIOUS FREEDOM IS ZULM

Minority non-Muslims should have the freedom to practice their religion as long as they are peaceful. When the Prophet[PBUH] took over as the ruler of Medina, he made a treaty (also known as the Constitution of Medina) with the Medina residents. In the context of the diversity, tolerance, and freedom of religion, he added the clause to the treaty: "The Jews follow their own faith, and Muslims follow their own faith."[78]

Similarly, the Prophet[PBUH] gave religious freedom to Christians of Najran (see above heading "Not Guilty by Association").

These statements are in line with the Quran, **"There is no compulsion in religion"** (2:256).

ZULM ON COMBATANT ENEMY

After the Prophet[PBUH] became head of the state of Medina, Muslims had to defend themselves against attacking Meccan pagans multiple times. Even if the pagans were the fiercest enemies of Muslims, Prophet Muhammad[PBUH] gave detailed instructions to Muslims to avoid zulm, both on the battlefield and inside enemy territory. Here are some highlights:[79]

- Do not torture anyone with fire.
- Do not attack any wounded person.
- Do not kill prisoners of war.
- No one should be tied down to be killed.
- Do not loot and destroy the enemy country.
- Muslims are prohibited from taking anything from the people of a conquered country without paying for it.
- Do not mutilate the corpses of a combatant enemy.
- If the enemy requests, return the dead body of their deceased.
- *Never breach a treaty.*
- Before attacking a state, openly declare war.

ZULM ON NON-COMBATANT ENEMY

The Prophet[PBUH] instructed, "Do not kill any old person, any child or any woman"[80] and "Do not kill monks in the monasteries…Muslims have been prohibited from taking anything from the general public of a conquered country without paying for it. If a Muslim army occupies an area of an enemy country, it does not have the right to use the things belonging to the people without their consent. If the army needs anything, they should purchase it."[81]

UNIVERSAL JUSTICE FOR ALL

Islam challenges the suffocating mindset of tribal and racial prejudice. Instead, Allah judges all humans based on their *beliefs and actions*. The Prophet[PBUH] emphasized in his famous last sermon: "All mankind is from Adam and Eve, an Arab has no superiority over a non-Arab nor a non-Arab has any superiority over an Arab; also a white has no superiority over a black nor a black has any superiority over white except by piety and good action."*[82]*

Likewise, Islam does not consider wealthy people superior and the poor inferior. Everyone is entitled to the same rights and should treat others with respect and kindness.

In Islam, universal love and racial equality are not just a theoretical concept. The Prophet[PBUH] implemented these principles in practice. For example, Bilal was an African who was enslaved in Mecca. He became Muslim and was severely tortured by the pagans. A companion, Abu-Bakr (who later became the first guided Caliph), purchased Bilal from his master and freed him. Later, Bilal moved to Medina with the Prophet[PBUH]. He noticed that Bilal was a pious, humble, and righteous man. The Prophet[PBUH] assigned him two very respected and responsible positions. Bilal was appointed as custodian of the treasury. In addition, he was given the highly prestigious duty of calling Adhan (call to assemble for prayer) five times a day.[83]

This is just one of many examples demonstrating that the Prophet[PBUH] was entirely free from any form of prejudice or bigotry. He envisioned all of humanity as one family and taught Companions the same.

ZULM OF DOMESTIC VIOLENCE

Domestic violence encompasses more than intimate partner abuse. It also includes violence against children and the elderly. There are many forms of domestic violence. According to South African freelance writer Ferguson, "Domestic violence can take many forms, including physical, sexual, emotional, financial, technological, and psychological abuse."[84]All of these forms of abuse are zulm because they not only ruin short-term relationships but also have the potential to cause long-lasting physical and psychological damage. It is essential to recognize and address domestic violence to prevent its escalation.

According to the National Center for Biotechnology Information Paper, "Family and domestic violence is a common problem in the United States, affecting an estimated 10 million people every year; as many as one in four women and one in nine men are victims of domestic violence."[85]

The positive news is that, in most cases, *unconditional love can play a crucial role in preventing domestic violence.*

One common cause of domestic violence is the desire to control, exploit, dominate, or manipulate the victim. Instead of such damaging behavior, if *aggression is replaced by unconditional love*, the violence and suffering are bound to subside. In domestic violence, both the aggressor and the victim belong to the same family. Therefore, it is easy to love a family member unconditionally.

Picture a scenario where a husband tries to ensure his wife's faithfulness and loyalty by using verbal or physical dominance and constant criticism. In this case, instead of resorting to physical or mental abuse, the most effective approach is to use unconditional love to communicate and openly address concerns about loyalty with the wife. When unconditional love is included in a relationship, can you imagine how much the situation will improve? Such an environment fosters loving communication, cooperation, and easy problem resolution. Respect and understanding are essential to a successful and loyal relationship. The husband should openly and honestly communicate his concerns to the wife. Simultaneously, he should listen to his wife and try to understand her feelings. If relevant, he should also apologize and take responsibility for his past actions. This will lead to a mutual agreement, which is comfortable for both partners. Eventually, life will become easier for the *whole family* (also see Chapter 1, heading "Islam-Inspired Love and Marriage").

All the arguments mentioned are equally applicable if the husband is a victim of any form of domestic oppression.

The Quran emphasizes that the relationship between a husband and wife should be one of peace and mutual support. If not, *both* should make a sincere effort towards this goal:

People, fear your Lord who created you from a single soul (4:1).

Spouses are garments for one another (2:187).

One of Allah's signs is that He created mates for you from yourselves so that you may find rest in them, and He put between you love and compassion; most surely, there are signs in this for people who reflect (30:21).

We can learn a lot from the Prophet's[PBUH] character: "(Prophet's[PBUH] wife) A'isha reported that the Prophet[PBUH] never beat anyone with his hand, neither a woman nor a servant, but only when he fought in the cause of Allah [Jihad]."[86]

In Islam, both committing zulm against others and voluntarily enduring zulm are considered serious sins. Please do not take domestic violence lightly. If necessary, seek professional help.

POINTS DISCUSSED SO FAR

It is truly remarkable to observe the level of precision with which Islam prohibits zulm in all aspects of human interactions. Zulm cannot be used against anyone, including children, elderly parents, employees, employers, on or off the battlefield, or animals. Muslims are fully responsible for those under their care, including non-Muslims. Believers should not waste natural resources. All courts of law should always uphold justice. A person's religion, social status, or familial relationship to the judge should never influence the judge's decision or lead to injustice.

The list goes on. An oppressed person is allowed complete freedom of speech to speak up against the oppressor. Any variation of domestic violence is also zulm. Courts must consistently implement full justice regardless of the judge's religion or family relationships. No one stands above the law. Muslim religious scholars and rulers are prohibited from committing any form of zulm. The end result of all actions, including actions that Islam recommends, must be just and fair.

The most surprising aspect is how immaculately Islam guides believers to refrain from harming *themselves* physically, emotionally, financially, and even while performing religious rituals. Islam prohibits bad habits (like gambling) and protects privacy at an individual level. The believers are prohibited from supporting a zalim leader. Thus, Islam guides the believers from perpetrating or experiencing any form of zulm. Only Allah's Book can codify so many details to eradicate zulm in all areas of our lives.

CONCLUSION

Why did Allah emphasize abstaining from zulm towards everyone, including zulm, against one's own self? Because Allah loves us, as in the verse, **"He [Allah] is the All-forgiving, the Most Loving One"** (85:14). We understand that simultaneously Allah tests us through various challenges (see Chapter 1, I am ugly, so I do not deserve love). However, the purpose of the tests is not to cause suffering. Instead, under the guidance from the Quran and hadith, committed believers are expected to learn and grow through hardships and difficulties to achieve *Nafs-e-Mutma'inna* in this life. In doing so, we also qualify to enter paradise. Thus, Allah desires our happiness, peace, and contentment in both this world and the afterlife.

Sufi Al-Junayd of Baghdad said:

> Thus it is that for your sake God protects you from yourself and causes
> you to pass by obliteration to eternal life so that you achieve your desire
> and live eternally with Him.[87]

AFTER THE PROPHET^{PBUH}, DID MUSLIMS CONTINUE TO UPHOLD THEIR COMMITMENT TO JUSTICE?

With so much emphasis on avoiding zulm, Muslims should be the most peace-loving, humane, just, and conscientious people in the world. Most Muslims certainly avoided zulm during the time of Prophet Muhammad^{PBUH} and the four guided caliphs (Abu-Bakr, Umar, Usman, and Ali). Here is one example:

During the reign of Caliph Ali, a Jew stole his armor. The caliph was also the highest legal judge at that time. To ensure impartiality and fairness, the case of theft was referred to a lower court judge instead of Caliph Ali's court. The judge asked Caliph Ali to produce witnesses to prove that the armor originally belonged to him. Caliph Ali produced his two sons and his slave as witnesses. The judge rejected the testimony of both sons, as they were too closely related to Caliph Ali. As a result, Caliph Ali failed to prove the case of theft.

The highest judge and ruler of the Muslims failed to prove his own case in a lower court. Islam prohibits punishing a suspect unless they are proven guilty beyond any doubt. The Jew was so impressed with the honesty and fairness of Muslims that he converted to Islam.[88] Several examples prove how Muslims in that era avoided zulm at all costs.

Islamic Teaching and Present-Day Muslims

How can we evaluate the commitment of present-day Muslim societies to refrain from zulm? One way would be to study the level of *corruption* in Muslim-majority countries. Corruption is a crime that undermines the public's trust in the government and erodes the public's faith in the fairness of the system. Undoubtedly, every type of corruption is unjust and zulm. If a country has a significant majority of honest citizens, its level of corruption is likely to decrease.

To initiate our analysis, we can consult the Transparency Index developed by Transparency International, which assesses the extent of corruption in various countries (www.transparency.org/en/cpi/2023). According to the index, Denmark ranks as the most honest nation in the world. It is sad to notice that among the top 25 most honest countries, there is not a single Muslim-majority country. The United Arab Emirates (UAE) is the most honest Muslim-majority country, ranking at number 26 on the index.

At this crossroads, we have two options:

OPTION A: We can ignore the Muslim corruption problem by claiming that people of all religions commit zulm and injustice. Therefore, Muslims are no exception. The advantage of this approach is that individual Muslims *deny the problem* exists. Therefore, Muslims are not responsible for providing the solution.

OPTION B: let us approach the same problem from a different point of view! There are about 50 Muslim-majority nations. Considering Islam's overemphasis on refraining from zulm, why are not all 50 Muslim-majority nations the most honest and fair? Ideally, all 50 Muslim-majority countries should be ranked *above* Denmark. This question remains valid even if Muslim nations are backward and poor. Many Prophet's[PBUH] companions were very poor, but still, they were profoundly honest.

Option B has two advantages (1) We acknowledge that the problem of corruption exists among Muslim nations. (2) Once we acknowledge the problem, we will be in a position to suggest a solution to the problem.

Corruption hurts the vast majority of the population. As a result, over the past several decades, millions of Muslims have migrated to Western nations. The irony is that once they settle there, most of the migrated Muslims eventually learn to be as honest as the population of the host country and live with less zulm.

SURPRISE – RAPE *VICTIMS* (NOT THE RAPISTS) WERE PUNISHED!!

So far, we have discussed how strongly Islam emphasizes justice and discourages zulm. Here are a few recent examples that show how some Muslims ignored the above teachings and practiced zulm. *The goal is only to acknowledge that the problem exists. Later, we will discuss a practical and peaceful solution.*

In 2001, Zafran Bibi of Pakistan filed a police complaint that her brother-in-law raped her. Here comes a surprise—the Pakistani court sentenced *her* to death by stoning. After she spent more than a year in jail, under international pressure, the court finally acquitted her in 2002. No charges were filed against the brother-in-law.

In 2001, a Northern Nigerian rape victim, Safiya Husaini, was convicted of having an illicit sexual relationship, and a local Islamic court sentenced her to death by stoning. Fortunately, she was later acquitted after a retrial.[89]

What if an unmarried rape victim chooses to avoid punishment by not reporting? That can also backfire if she becomes pregnant. A divorced Bangladeshi woman was raped and became pregnant. In 2006, she was sentenced to be struck 101 times with a cane because the pregnancy of an unmarried woman was sure proof of sex out of wedlock.[90]

BACKGROUND OF ADULTERY PUNISHMENT

A companion of the Prophet came home and saw that his wife was having sex with another man. The husband went to the Prophet[PBUH] to complain. The Prophet[PBUH] asked the husband to prove his accusation of *zina* (adultery) by producing four male witnesses who *simultaneously* saw the sexual act. The husband said that was an impossible condition. Still, the Prophet insisted that without producing four witnesses, the husband would face punishment for slander. This rule aims to protect women from the zulm of false accusations.

At that time, several verses of chapter 24 of the Quran were revealed to the Prophet[PBUH]. According to the verses, if four eyewitnesses support the charge of adultery, *only then* will both the adulterous man and woman get caned 100 times. I support the opinion that severe punishment points to the seriousness of the sin of adultery and fornication. However, the nearly impossible condition of securing four genuine witnesses makes the crime of adultery practically unpunishable in this world.

What about the husband who witnessed the scene and was going through emotional trauma or zulm? The Quran also provided a way to get divorced. If the husband chooses, he can accuse the wife of adultery in court and take an oath that he is speaking the truth. After that, the wife can accept guilt or deny the charge under oath. If she denies the charge, the court will declare her *not guilty* and *annul the marriage*.[91] In either case, the lying party will be punished on the Day of Judgment. However, it must be noted that the adultery incident had nothing to do with rape.

The problem started when Muslim scholars defined *"Zina* a lot more liberally, where *zina* means *adultery, fornication, prostitution, and rape."*[92] The inclusion of rape with adultery also carried with it the impossible condition of four male eyewitnesses. This had devastating consequences. "For almost 30 years, hundreds of women in Pakistan were incriminated and charged with the offense of zina as they inevitably failed to prove rape charges."[93] Pakistani police have proved to be disappointingly immoral in practice by refusing to register cases under … rape and recording instead as cases of *Zina* (i.e., adultery).[94]

The author of this book thinks that *Zina* is not the same as rape. Because legally speaking, there is no similarity between the above incident of zina and rape! *Zina* or adultery is an offense when the husband/society/government accuses a woman of having *consensual* immoral sex. So, the husband or someone else is the accuser/plaintiff, and the *woman is the accused*. Whereas rape is a crime in which a woman accuses a man of sexual abuse. So, *the woman is the accuser/plaintiff,* and the man is the accused. These are two entirely different circumstances. *Zina* is consensual sex, but rape is undoubtedly non-consensual. In *zina,* a woman is punished for *choosing* adultery, while a rape victim has no choice.

Allah forgave women who were *forced* into prostitution because they were *victims.* When a woman is raped or forced to have sex, she becomes a helpless victim. How can she be accused of *consensual sex* or adultery? Before approving penal laws, those in favor should thoroughly consider all possibilities to ensure the law does not lead to zulm. Furthermore, the law should take into account any potential unintended consequences or repercussions. It therefore makes no sense to impose the *zina* witness requirement, and punishment, on the rape victim. Furthermore, it fails to take into account the trauma that the victim has experienced and does not provide justice. This is zulm, without a doubt.

It must have been traumatic for Pakistani women to realize that if they get raped, they will be blamed for promiscuity and put behind bars. Such laws create a culture of fear and silence, where many victims are afraid to report the crime. In addition, people all over the world blame Islam for cruelty and injustice. Many Muslims (*yes, Muslims*) leave Islam.

> **NOTE:** The words Islam and Muslim are not synonyms. Islam is a religion, while a Muslim is a person who claims to follow the religion of Islam.

WHAT DO ISLAMIC HOLY BOOKS SAY ABOUT RAPE?

There are two primary sources of Islamic information: the Quran and *hadith*. What do these two sources say about rape? The Quran does not discuss rape. However, the following hadith acquits the rape victim without the need for four witnesses: "A slave was in charge of the slaves in the khumus, and he forced a slave-girl among those slaves against her will and had intercourse with her. Umar ibn al-Khattab had him flogged and banished him, and he did not flog the slave girl because the slave had forced her."[95] In the context of rape, the hadith does not support the requirement of four witnesses to establish the innocence of the rape victim. Furthermore, the raped victim was not penalized.

A position paper by *KARAMA* titled "Zina, Rape, and Islamic Law: an Islamic legal analysis of the rape laws in Pakistan" conclusively proves that the rape law imposed in Pakistan from 1979 to 2006 was incompatible with Islamic law. Why did Islamic scholars make and support such an absurd law? *It is a question for them.* Perhaps they did not fully understand the significance of zulm. No *dictionary meaning of the word rape can overrule the decree of Allah in the Quran that strictly prohibits zulm.*

There are many examples of oppression by contemporary Muslim scholars. In Nigeria, Pakistan, and Afghanistan, Muslim scholars banned polio vaccinations, causing immeasurable suffering and death. Before 1988, all over the world, an estimated 350,000 people were infected with polio, a virus that can cripple them for the rest of their lives.[96] How can any human allow so much suffering to innocents?

LATELY, WHY HAVE MUSLIMS EMBRACED ZULM?

The problem is obviously not with Islam itself. The problem lies with contemporary Muslim scholars. Some Muslim scholars refused to acknowledge that zulm is prohibited in Islam. They do not preach: *doing zulm on anyone (including yourself) is a sin.* They should not forget that Prophet Muhammad[PBUH] said, "All of you are guardians and are responsible for your subjects. The ruler is a guardian and responsible for his subjects; the man is a guardian of his family; the woman is a guardian in her husband's house and responsible for her wards; a servant is a guardian of his master's property and responsible for his wards."[97]

In summary, Muslims should always be fair and just in every walk of life. These rules establish the foundation of Muslim ethics and moral values. Ignoring these rules creates an ethical vacuum, leading to a lack of respect for other people, a lack of consideration for their rights, and ultimately, a lack of justice in society.

Muslim scholars occasionally discuss charity, caring for old parents, or helping the needy. But this is only a very narrow subset of the concept of zulm. For example, if you cut a line in a grocery store, you did zulm. If you take more food on your plate than you can possibly eat and trash the leftovers, then it is zulm. Muslim scholars rarely mention the overwhelming emphasis on zulm in *every aspect of human interaction*. You can easily verify this claim by browsing the Islamic books section of a library. Just pick up any book on Islam. There is a 95 percent chance that you will not find any reference to zulm at all. If, by a remarkable coincidence, you see a chapter that refers to zulm, then again, there is about a 95 percent chance that the book you picked up is *Islam: Path of Infinite Love!*

On a positive note, credit also goes to some Sufi teachings promoting love and justice. Sufi Al-Junayd said:

> The Sufi is like the earth, on which every foul thing is thrown and from which fair things come forth.[98]

The above quote says that even when faced with ill-treatment (zulm) from others, a pious Muslim should always respond with kindness and justice. This demonstrates the strength of their faith and their commitment to justice. It also encourages others to create a more peaceful and harmonious society.

IHSAN: ISLAM RAISES THE STANDARD OF JUSTICE

Haqooq ul Ibad refers to the Islamic principle of practicing justice and avoiding zulm in all social interactions. It is the minimum duty of every Muslim toward other humans. However, according to Islam, there is more. A Muslim unconditionally loves Allah. Inspired by love, a Muslim may do something *extra*, something nice for Allah's creation. A loving mother not only feeds and clothes her baby (the minimum requirement to keep the child alive), but she does much more in caring for, loving, and trying to make everything comfortable for the baby. Her motivation is not duty, recognition, or money but unconditional love for the child. When a person not only fulfills his/her assigned Islamic duty but also voluntarily does more, it is called *ihsan*, the merging point of several Islamic virtues.

EXAMPLE OF IHSAN

The Quran says. **"Allah commands doing justice, doing *ihsan* to others and giving [charity] to relatives"** (16:90). Every good deed can be improved so that it becomes ihsan. The Prophet[PBUH] said, "Verily Allah has enjoined excellence (Ihsan) to everything."[99] The Quran explains: **"Do *Ihsan* to your parents, kinfolks, orphans, the helpless, near and far neighbors who keep company with you, the travelers in need, and the enslaved people you own. Allah does not love those who are arrogant and boastful"** (4:36).

When Prophet Muhammad[PBUH] was the ruler of Medina and was surrounded by many companions, a desert Arab approached him and pulled his and *Rida'* (sheet) so hard that the Prophet's[PBUH] neck turned red. The desert Arab aggressively demanded, "O Muhammad[PBUH]! Order for me some of Allah's property which you have." At that time, the Prophet could have punished the Arab for his aggression or at least told him how to behave. Instead, Prophet Muhammad[PBUH] lovingly smiled and gave him charity.[100] This is *Ihsan*. Consider the possible repercussions if someone treated a head of state in the same manner today.

EMPHASIS ON *IHSAN*

The Quran puts an overwhelming emphasis on ihsan. Allah promises a reward for ihsan on the Day of Judgment: **"Is there any reward for Ihsan other than Ihsan?"** (55:60). In verses 2:195, 3:134, 3:148, 5:13, and 5:93, the Quran repeats five times: **"Allah *loves* those who do *ihsan*"** (5:93). To those who strive on the path of ihsan, Allah promises His help in the form of wisdom and knowledge, right in this life, just as Allah helped Prophet Joseph[PBUH]: **"We [Allah] bestowed on him wisdom and knowledge. Thus, We reward those who do *ihsan*"** (12:22).

Ihsan also has another benefit in this life. Since Ihsan is based on the unconditional love of Allah, therefore, after you do ihsan to someone, you are guaranteed to feel peace and joy. *This is an essential side effect of unconditional love.* You can easily verify this by doing Ihsan. Ibn Qayyim al-Jawziyya said:

> If you do not find sweetness and joy in the deed [of ihsan] you perform, then doubt its sincerity.[101]

Rumi said:

> When you do things from your soul, you feel a river moving in you, a joy.[102]

HOW MANY TIMES DOES THE WORD *JIHAD* APPEAR IN THE QURAN?

Radicals overemphasize the concept of *jihad*, which has multiple meanings, including war. While the word *jihad* appears 41 times in the Quran, on only 12 occasions, it is used to mean war. Islamic scholar Ahmed Al-Dawoody presented a detailed breakdown of its usage: *Seventeen derivatives of jihād occur altogether forty-one times in eleven Meccan texts and thirty Medinan ones, with the following five meanings: striving because of religious belief (21),* **war (12)** *non-Muslim parents exerting pressure, that is, jihād, to make their children abandon Islam (2), solemn oaths (5) and physical strength (1)* [103].

Here, we see that the Quran uses the word *jihad* (war) several times less than the word *zulm* (to discourage oppression). *This proves a severe error in incorrectly assigning priorities.*

HOW TO GUIDE TODAY'S MUSLIMS BACK TO JUSTICE?

Our goal is not to insult or humiliate Muslim scholars who have ignored zulm. Why? *An unnecessary offense against anyone is zulm.* Besides, personal verbal attacks are unlikely to be effective. After the four rightly guided caliphs, several Muslim rulers adopted repressive policies. Unlike today, back then, Muslims considered avoiding zulm as a fundamental part of Islam. The public used to ask state officials: "Why do you practice such barbarities [zulm]? Is not all this against the spirit of Islam? Are you not Muslims?"[104] Even if the above questions made sense, directly accusing someone of not being Muslim is offensive. That approach failed to change the course of history.

Proposed Solution

How do we *politely* convey the significance of zulm to Muslim scholars? Our goal is not only to tell them to avoid zulm in their own lives but also to teach Muslims to avoid zulm. This book proposes the following two-step solution:

Step 1: Let us follow the guidance in the Quran. When Allah commanded Prophet Moses[PBUH] to go and guide Pharaoh, then Prophet Moses[PBUH] prayed: **"O my Lord!** *Open my chest* **[so I make spiritual progress**

and] make my task easy" (20:25–26). So, the first step is to *change one's own self*. If you wish to teach justice to others, you must first practice justice yourself in every area of human interaction. That means avoiding doing zulm on others and yourself.

Step 2: Again, let us follow the guidance in the Quran: **"Strive against them with this *Quran*, a *mighty* Jihad [strenuous striving]"** (25:52). The Quran is not a weapon, it is a book of guidance. As a solution, let us use the Quranic teachings and *peacefully* communicate the message of justice. Instead of aggressively accusing the scholars of being wrong, we will only point to their errors. The evidence is overwhelmingly in our favor.

"Appendix A" of this book lists the 288 verses of the Quran that condemn zulm. It also presents questions that will compel Islamic scholars to reassess their thinking. You can give a copy of Appendix A to any Muslim scholar who writes about or preaches Islam. If several people do this after every Friday congregational prayer, soon the scholars will realize that Islam does not support zulm. *Our peaceful preaching can change the behavior of Muslims all over the world.* Do not underestimate the power of Islam.

Do no zulm, and you will not be subjected to zulm (Quran 2:279)

CHAPTER 3

SURPRISE: THE FIRST MAJOR PEACEFUL TRANSFER OF POWER IN HISTORY

S ome scholars credit America for the first peaceful transfer of power. "Peaceful transfer of power from one party to another that occurred in the United States—the first such transfer of power in history."[105] But this statement is not true. More than a thousand years earlier, Prophet Muhammad[PBUH] took over power in Medina *without any bloodshed*.

The Prophet's[PBUH] unprecedented large-scale peaceful power transfer was a remarkable accomplishment that exceeded all expectations. By no means can this achievement be considered typical or mundane. It is a testament to the Prophet's[PBUH] exceptional foresight, skill, and wisdom. Let us take into account the following challenging odds he was up against:

1. The residents of Medina were not all Muslims. At that time, Medina was a multi-religious society consisting of the polytheists of Medina, Jews, and Muslims.[106]

2. Prophet Muhammad[PBUH] did not inherit power through a dynasty.

3. He belonged to a tribe different from the people of Medina, which was a crucial factor for the Arabs. For thousands of years, they had a tradition of ruler succession based on tribal affiliations.

4. When the Prophet[PBUH] took over the power in Medina, *he did not even have an army*. During almost all of his journey from Mecca to Medina to assume power, he was accompanied only by one person, Abu-Bakr.

5. Prophet Muhammad[PBUH] was not even a citizen of the city of Medina. He came from Mecca, which was a city-state governed by a different administration. So, *it was just like a foreigner taking over as head of state*.

6. At that time, Medina was wracked by generations-old inter-tribal civil war between the tribes of Banu Aus and Banu Khazraj. The Prophet[PBUH] had such a good reputation that both tribes almost unanimously accepted Prophet Muhammad[PBUH] as their leader.

Upon his arrival in Medina, the Prophet[PBUH] accomplished an incredible feat by bringing peace between these two warring Arab tribes, thus ending the civil war. It was an outstanding accomplishment that left everyone in awe of his wisdom and leadership. The Prophet[PBUH] also made peace agreements with Jews.

The entire city celebrated his arrival by singing a famous song that is still popular today. Though there was some political opposition, even in such a war-torn environment, there was *absolutely no violence.*

Though they did not have voting like modern democracies, the enthusiastic participation of nearly the entire diverse population in welcoming the Prophet[PBUH] and the absence of violent opposition demonstrated his popularity.

When Thomas Jefferson was elected president of the United States, only property owners/taxpaying[107] white men were allowed to vote. Women and enslaved people were not allowed to cast their votes.

7. Prophet Muhammad[PBUH] did not execute political opponents of Medina and allowed them complete freedom of speech, provided they were nonviolent. After taking power in Medina, his rule was threatened by a political opponent, Abdullah bin Ubai, who had many followers. He did not openly revolt against the Prophet[PBUH] because almost the entire population supported the Prophet[PBUH]. Instead, he tried overthrowing the Prophet's rule through conspiracies and secret plots. One of Ubai's most aggressive actions was taken during the Battle of Uhud. Ubai and his followers pretended to be Muslims. They traveled with the Prophet[PBUH] and other Muslims to the battleground to face the aggressive army of Mecca's pagans.

However, right before the battle, Ubai and his 300 followers walked back to Medina, leaving only 700 Muslims to face a 3,000-strong, well-equipped pagan army. Besides reducing the headcount, his action hurt Muslim morale. Ubai persistently tried to overthrow the Prophet[PBUH] and, in doing so, hurt Muslims. Still, Prophet

Muhammad[PBUH] did not persecute Ubai but allowed him complete freedom of speech. Abdullah bin Ubai remained an active political opponent until his death. The Prophet's[PBUH] example serves as a reminder of the power of diplomacy and negotiation.

This raises an intriguing question: *Has there ever been a historical instance where a foreigner peacefully assumed control of a nation against similar odds (considering that the Prophet[PBUH] was not even a citizen of Medina)?* His achievement is even more impressive because he accomplished it during an ongoing civil war between two Medina tribes.

How about in the future? *Realistically speaking, can we imagine anyone in the future peacefully becoming the head of state under similar odds?*

THE SECRETS OF THE "PEACEFUL TRANSFER OF POWER"

The Prophet[PBUH] was not a mythological or imaginary character. He was a real person who has been recorded in history. This means we can learn a lot by studying his personality, decisions, and achievements. The following section will explore the factors that contributed to the unprecedented achievement of history's first large-scale peaceful transfer of power.

Earning Public Trust

Before claiming power, the Prophet[PBUH] established a solid reputation as an honest and wise person who always pursued justice and avoided zulm at all costs. People of Mecca nicknamed him *al-Ameen* (the Trustworthy).

<u>Leadership Qualities</u>

When the Prophet[PBUH] was 35 years old (five years before he was assigned the responsibilities of the prophethood), a dispute erupted among the leaders of Arab clans. The incident occurred when the revered building *Kaba*, located in Mecca, was being renovated. The Arabs especially valued a stone of Kaba called *the black stone*. Each tribal chief desired the honor of manually placing the black stone in its rightful place in the building of Kaba. According to the custom of that era, such disputes could have resulted in long-lasting hostility and even loss of lives. To peacefully resolve the situation, tribal leaders unanimously elected Muhammad[PBUH] as an arbitrator. The tribal leaders said, "Al-Ameen (the trustworthy) has come. We are content to abide by his decision."[108]

63

Among the many tribal chiefs, choosing a specific leader to place the Black Stone in its rightful position was a challenging dilemma. Regardless of who was selected, it would have caused resentment among the other tribes. Muhammad[PBUH] suggested a wise and unusual solution: he asked for a large sheet of cloth. Then, he placed the black stone in the middle of the cloth. Next, he asked each tribal chief to hold on to one corner of the sheet. Thus, they *all* carried the black stone near its designated place. Then, he placed the stone where it was supposed to go. Thus, the problem was *permanently and peacefully* resolved.[109]

This incident provides valuable understanding about the Prophet's[PBUH] personality:
1. The Prophet[PBUH] had such a prestigious reputation that all tribal chiefs trusted his judgment and wisdom. They unanimously selected him to arbitrate such a sensitive issue. This provides significant insight into his personality and public image.
2. Even if the Prophet[PBUH] grew up in deep-rooted tribal culture, his thinking transcended tribal prejudice. He did not think along the lines of promoting his own tribe to get the approval of his tribe members. Instead, his out-of-the-box thinking was directed at justice, unity, and mutual cooperation. His goal was to seek a peaceful and acceptable solution and avoid conflicts.

He was a True Gentleman and a Conscientious Person
His wife Khadija described the Prophet as "A person who is kind to his relatives, speaks only the truth, helps the poor, orphans, and people in need, and is an honest man."[110] Many incidents attest to the above statement. His motto was to help the entire human race, not just Muslims. The Quran cares about the needy regardless of religion: "**Feed the poor, the orphan, and the prisoners for the love of Allah**" (76:8).

He Did Not Abandon the Muslims of Mecca

When the Prophet[PBUH] started to preach Islam, the pagans of Mecca began to mercilessly oppress Muslims, including the Prophet[PBUH]. Despite the danger posed by the pagans of Mecca, the Prophet[PBUH] chose not to leave the Muslims behind and relocate alone to a safer city. Instead, he remained steadfast in Mecca, even when his own life was at risk. All along, he was looking for a solution for all Muslims, not just for himself. Thus, the

Prophet^{PBUH} demonstrated his selflessness, commitment, honesty, and sincerity.

Word of mouth established his reputation as a fair, dedicated, and impartial leader throughout Medina and the surrounding communities. Consequently, the people of Medina wholeheartedly welcomed his rule. Not a drop of blood was shed.

Immediately upon reaching Medina, he not only reconciled two warring Medina tribes but also established peace treaties with various Jewish tribes near Medina. He even consulted his subjects on essential issues. The Quran ranks *consultation* as a praise-worthy act: **"[Those] who have pledged their obedience to the Lord, …*who conduct their affairs with consultation among themselves*"** (42:38). Here we catch a glimpse of another aspect of the Prophet's character; he favored cooperation, coexistence, and collaboration with others rather than dividing or imposing his will on them forcefully.

By Planning Ahead, He Prevented Several Future Problems
The desert town of Medina had depleted resources, including a very limited water supply. Nonetheless, Prophet Muhammad^{PBUH} made sure that Muslims migrating from Mecca were given *shelter and respectable status* in society. From any perspective, this was an extraordinary achievement. He lived in peace with the Jewish tribes until they broke the agreement.

ADMINISTRATIVE CAPABILITIES OF THE PROPHET^{PBUH}

During Times of Calamity, He Displayed Remarkable Wisdom

The migration of Prophet Muhammad^{PBUH} and the Muslims to Medina, unfortunately, caused a new problem for the people of Medina — the enmity of the overwhelmingly powerful and resourceful pagans of Mecca. Their armies attacked Medina several times. Abdullah bin Ubai and his followers raised serious concerns about this new animosity of the Pagans from Mecca. However, Prophet Muhammad^{PBUH} used his negotiating skills and foresight to peacefully avoid any domestic conflict in Medina. *Nonviolently*, he managed to restrain Abdullah bin Ubai. The Prophet^{PBUH} did not wage jihad to solve every problem. After Prophet Muhammad^{PBUH} took over power, overall violence significantly decreased because he stopped the ongoing civil war between the two main tribes of Medina. After the Battle of Hunain, the original residents of Medina unanimously agreed that they were far better off after the migration of the Muslims from Mecca.[111]

He only Fought Defensive Battles

When the Prophet[PBUH] was head of the state of Medina, Mecca's pagans attacked Muslims many times. The three most significant pagan attacks on Muslims resulted in the Battle of Badr, the Battle of Uhud, and the Battle of the Trench. Indian scholar Geragh Ali pointed out that the battleground of Badr is very close to the city of Medina, where Prophet Muhammad[PBUH] lived with the Muslims. This proves that *the pagan army must have started several days earlier and almost reached Medina, where the Muslims came out to defend their city.* Therefore, it is evident that the pagans were the aggressors and *Muslims were defending themselves.*[112] Similarly, Uhud's battleground is also very close to the city of Medina. In the battle of Trenches, the pagan army surrounded the city of Medina, and Muslims dug a trench to protect the city. Therefore, *all three battles were fought in defense* against pagan attacks. According to Islamic scholar Fatoohi:

> "Armed jihad [in Islam] is a *defensive reaction* rather than an offensive action."[113]

After the conquest of Mecca in 630 CE, the problem of pagan animosity was solved (with the least amount of violence), and the Prophet[PBUH] became the ruler of Medina, Mecca, and the surrounding areas; he received news that the neighboring Byzantine (Roman) Empire was preparing to attack the Muslim rule. In defense, the Prophet[PBUH] put together a large volunteer Muslim army and traveled to the edge of the Roman empire to a place called Tabuk. However, the Roman army did not show up. This was an ideal opportunity for any aggressive conqueror to seize land without facing resistance and expand their territory. What did the Prophet[PBUH] do? Instead of attacking the Roman land, after waiting for 20 days, the Prophet[PBUH] *retreated the Muslim army back to Medina.* Why did he not occupy unprotected Roman lands? When the Roman army failed to appear, they ceased to be an immediate threat, so there was no longer any justification to attack the Roman lands. *This proves that the Prophet[PBUH] engaged only in defensive battles.*

During his 20-day stay in Tabuk, many non-Muslim neighboring tribes made peace agreements with him. During that period, the Roman Empire was under Christian leadership. British-American historian Bernard Lewis, who specialized in Oriental studies, explained that even non-Muslims preferred Prophet's[PBUH] rule to Byzantine rule because the new yoke was far lighter than the old, both in taxation and in other matters. Some, even among the Christian population of Syria and Egypt, preferred the rule of Islam.[114] Why were Muslims so fair to the people they ruled? The explanation is obvious: back then, *Muslims practiced justice and refrained from doing zulm on anyone.*

LESSONS FOR MUSLIM LEADERS IN 21ST CENTURY

Today's Muslim political leaders can learn many lessons from the Prophet's[PBUH] life. The first and foremost lesson is that the Prophet[PBUH] was *not* constantly at war or attacking others. Instead, the Prophet[PBUH] fought only *defensive* wars or participated in preemptive strikes to avoid an imminent enemy attack. He did not attack anyone without a proper justification. He did not attack peaceful non-Muslims. For example, instead of attacking the pagans from Mecca, the Prophet[PBUH] made a peace treaty with them (described in the next Chapter).

Today, to effectively rule a nation, Muslim leaders should also begin by serving as *social workers* and, just like the Prophet[PBUH], demonstrate their ability to manage and serve through small-scale practical examples. Emulating the Prophet[PBUH], they should prioritize peacefully winning public opinion over engaging in jihad and causing destruction.

In the 21ˢᵗ century, like everyone else, Muslims also depend on modern necessities and comforts. The sad reality is that Muslims have ended up in a contradictory state of simultaneously *rejecting and depending on modernism.* According to Nobel Laureate author VS Naipaul, this is "the confusion of a people [Muslims] of high medieval culture awakening to oil and money, a sense of power and violation and a knowledge of a great new encircling civilization. <u>That civilization could not be mastered. It was to be rejected; at the same time, it was to be depended on.</u>"[115]

21ˢᵗ-century leaders should acknowledge that Muslim masses hopelessly depend on modern conveniences like cell phones, hospitals, computers, robots, drones, cars, water purifying plants, planes, electricity, the internet, medicines, AI, and so on. Only a few Muslim-majority nations are modernizing. However, they are not the global leaders in research, manufacturing, innovation, education, personal freedom, and governance.

The political systems in those countries are not well-established enough to facilitate periodic peaceful transfers of power.

Muslims cannot afford to reject constructive changes. The *Muslim leadership should embrace modernity and welcome positive changes with open arms!* Muslim political parties should strive to *minimize zulm in all aspects of life.* To provide jobs in today's overpopulated world and satisfactorily raise the standard of living, political parties should plan to implement *modern* education, industrialization, healthcare, and economic development. They should also build infrastructure and look after the poorest segment of society. *To minimize zulm,* the government should protect women's rights, the rights of the physically and mentally challenged, and the rights of religious and racial minorities. Everyone should have full freedom of speech (Chapter 2, heading "Freedom of Speech Against Zulm").

If this can be accomplished, just like at the time of the Prophet[PBUH], the power can still be transferred peacefully without violent conflict.

Muslims have ended up in a paradoxical situation where they simultaneously reject and depend on modernism.

CHAPTER 4

THE PEACE TREATY OF al-HUDAYBIA

BACKGROUND

Prophet Abraham[PBUH] and his son raised the foundation of Kaba in Mecca (verse 2:127) and preached monotheism to the local Arabs. Several centuries later, in 610 CE, by the time Prophet Muhammad[PBUH] was assigned the duties of the Prophethood, the Arabs practiced a corrupted version of religion. They forgot many teachings of Prophet Abraham[PBUH]. Mecca became a hub of polytheistic worship, with numerous idols housed in the Kaba. Pagan Arabs worshipped different gods and goddesses along with Allah. They regarded prophet Abraham[PBUH] as their patriarch and visited the revered building *Kaba* for pilgrimage. Muslims regard Abraham[PBUH] as a prophet, and similar to pagan Arabs, Muslims consider the Kaba as their holiest site.

For centuries, the pagans in Mecca regarded the area surrounding the Kaba as a holy sanctuary. Inside the sanctuary, every tribe was allowed to make the pilgrimage, regardless of whether the tribe was friendly or adversarial and regardless of which god or goddess they worshipped. After the Muslims and Prophet Muhammad[PBUH] migrated to Medina, however, the pagans in Mecca singled out Muslims and prohibited them from entering Mecca, even for pilgrimage.

Two Options of "Defensive Jihad"

By the year 628 CE (about five years after the Prophet[PBUH] and most Muslims migrated to Medina), the pagan armies from Mecca had attacked Muslims in Medina on several occasions. In defense, the Muslims had to fight three major battles: the Battle of Badr (624 CE), the Battle of Uhud (626 CE), and the Battle of Trench (627 CE). After these battles, the Prophet[PBUH] had only two options left:

A. **Wait For the Next Major Pagan Attack**: In response, Muslims would be forced to fight another defensive battle. Rather than seeking peace, the Arab warrior tradition emphasized continuing the cycle of vengeance and engaging in extended conflicts. In addition, the pagans wanted their religion to dominate Islam. This meant that attacks would continue one after another until one side was almost annihilated. This option would have resulted in tremendous carnage on both sides.

B. **Attack the Pagans in Mecca**: Since the migration to Medina, the number of Muslims had been steadily increasing. Compared to previous years, Muslims were probably better positioned in 628 CE to attack the pagans in Mecca and seize control of the city. This, too, would have resulted in bloodshed on both sides.

Islam allows only defensive warfare. Therefore, both options mentioned above were permissible because Muslims were defending themselves against pagans who had been hostile towards them for the past fifteen years. *The Prophet*[PBUH] *rejected both options, A and B, because they involved violence.*

How to Solve a Problem Non-Violently?

Under Allah's guidance, the Prophet[PBUH] planned a nonviolent solution to avoid war by defying the ban on Muslim entry to Mecca to make the pilgrimage. The Prophet[PBUH] led a Muslim caravan of 1400 pilgrims from Medina to Mecca to perform Umrah (pilgrimage), an entirely peaceful activity. When the pagans learned the intention of the approaching Muslims, they dispatched a heavily armed unit of 200 horsemen to intercept the caravan and prevent the Muslims from entering Mecca. Rather than confronting the pagan army, the Prophet[PBUH] changed the caravan route.[116] Thus, he avoided another opportunity to wage a defensive jihad.

Finally, the Muslim caravan camped on the edge of the Kaba sanctuary zone at a place called Hudaybia. This created an unexpected problem for the pagans. According to English philosopher Martin Lings, "If they [Mecca's pagans], the guardians of the sanctuary, were to hinder the approach of over a thousand Arab pilgrims to the holy house [Kaba], this would be a most flagrant violation of the laws on which all their own greatness was founded." [117] The pagans tried to prove that the Muslims did not qualify for sanctuary status because they came with the intention to attack, but their own observers confirmed that the Muslims were made up of a peaceful caravan of pilgrims. This shows the beauty of Prophet Muhammad's[PBUH] strategy. *Even when fighting was justified, he tactfully avoided even defensive jihad and nonviolently forced the recalcitrant and powerful enemy to make peace.*

IN ISLAM, NEGOTIATION HAS A HIGHER PRIORITY THAN VIOLENCE

Next, the Prophet[PBUH] proposed a treaty, not just to make the pilgrimage but also *to end the animosity between the pagans and Muslims.* He proposed that the pagans and Muslims would not attack each other for the next ten years.

The pagans *had to* allow Muslims to perform the pilgrimage because the Prophet's[PBUH] remarkable strategy ruled out violence as an option for the pagans.

For pilgrimage, Muslims would have to travel to Kaba, located in Mecca. Therefore, pagan negotiator Suhayl ibn Amr also agreed to the suggested peace treaty to avoid potential confrontation. The second reason might be that, after confronting Muslims in battles multiple times, the pagans realized that defeating Muslims in battle was not an ordinary endeavor.

Suhayl ibn Amr, however, added an unfair condition that Muslims would not be permitted to perform the pilgrimage that year but could do so starting the following year.

Suhayl ibn Amr insisted on adding a clause about the extradition of refugees, which was highly prejudiced against Muslims. He insisted that Muslims would not give refuge to anyone from Mecca who escaped to Medina without his guardian's permission. Instead, Muslims would *hand that person back* to the pagans of Mecca. Conversely, if a person from Medina sought refuge with the pagans in Mecca, the pagans wouldn't be obligated to return them.

This condition was aimed at stopping further conversions to Islam, as the Prophet's[PBUH] teachings were profoundly moving and captivating, and people from various faiths were steadily embracing Islam. New converts often escaped to Medina to avoid pagan persecution. By adding the extradition condition, Suhayl ibn Amr threatened all potential converts with severe torture.

In addition, Suhail ibn Amr insisted that the treaty document should not state that Muhammad[PBUH] was a Prophet of Allah because pagans did not believe in his prophethood.

HOW DID THE COMPANIONS REACT TO THE TREATY?

For obvious reasons, most of the Companions were unhappy with the biased terms of the treaty. To most Muslims, it appeared that the Prophet[PBUH] made too many compromises and let the pagans interfere with the Islamic ritual of performing pilgrimage. Umar could not contain himself and discussed the doubts with the Prophet[PBUH]. Pakistani Islamic scholar Muhammad Shafi described the conversation between Omar and the Prophet[PBUH]:

Sayyidna Umar exclaimed in extreme grief and indignation: "0 Messenger of Allah! Are you not the True Prophet of Allah?"[118]
The Prophet[PBUH] replied: "Of course I am."
Then Sayyidna Umar asked, "Are we not on the right path, and are they on the wrong [path]?"[119]
The Prophet[PBUH] replied: "Of course, we are on the right path."
Sayyidna Umar asked: "Is it not a fact that our martyrs are in Paradise and their slain ones in the Fire?"[120]
The Prophet[PBUH] replied: "Yes, it is a fact."
Sayyidna Umar then said: "Why should we submit to this humiliation and return without observing Umrah or *Allah decides the matter through war*? [why do not we fight pagans and get better treaty terms?]."
The Messenger of Allah replied: "I am the servant of Allah and His Messenger. *I can never violate His command*. He will never destroy me. He is my Helper."[121]

Still, it was not apparent to most of the companions why the Prophet[PBUH] made so many concessions for the pagans, even when the pagans failed to dominate Muslims on the battlefields.

UNFORGETTABLE INCIDENT BEFORE SIGNING THE TREATY

While the treaty was being drafted, Suhail ibn Amr's son, Abu Jandal, arrived. He lived in Mecca and converted to Islam. As a result, he was cruelly tortured. Somehow, he managed to escape the captivity and joined Muslim pilgrims in Hudaybia to seek refuge. Let us keep in mind that many Companions, along with the Prophet[PBUH], had been victims of severe pagan torture. They felt deep compassion for Abu Jandal and tried to secure his freedom. But Suhail ibn Amr stood firm and insisted that " 'To signify that you are faithful to your contract, an opportunity has just arrived.' The Prophet[PBUH] said: 'But the treaty was not signed when your son entered the camp.' Upon this, he burst forth and said, 'But the terms of the treaty were agreed upon.' It was indeed an anxious moment. On the one hand, Abu Jandal was lamenting at the top of his voice, 'Am I to be returned to the polytheists that they might entice me from my religion, O Muslims!' But, on the other hand, the faithful engagement was also considered to be necessary, above all other considerations. The Prophet's[PBUH] heart welled up with sympathy, but he wanted to honor his word at all costs. He consoled Abu Jandal and said, 'Be patient, resign yourself to the Will of Allah. He is going to provide for you and your helpless companions relief and means of escape. We have concluded a *treaty of peace* with them, and we have made the pledge in the name of Allah. *We are, therefore, under no circumstances prepared to break it.* ' "[122] As a result, Abu Jandal was handed back to the pagans.

After the treaty was signed and finalized, the Prophet[PBUH] ordered the Companions to perform the pilgrimage rituals like shaving their heads and sacrificing the animals in Hudaybia instead of the designated locations near Kaba. The Companions were in such a shock that *no one obeyed him*. The Prophet[PBUH] retired to his tent where his wife Umm Salamah advised him: " 'Do not reprimand them at this time, because they are acutely grieved by the terms of the Treaty and by returning without observing Umrah. Call the barber in the presence of all, and get your own head shaved, put off your pilgrim garb, and slaughter your own camel.' He followed her advice. When the Companions saw this, they followed suit."[123] This incident shows the extent of dissatisfaction and disappointment among the Companions. Still, the Prophet[PBUH] remained focused on *peace* through the treaty and was not swayed by anyone's approval. Only a person who truly understands the importance of *peace* can maintain such confidence and determination.

HOW DID ALLAH RATE THE TREATY OF AL-HUDAYBIA?

The peace treaty was such a significant event that, shortly after the treaty was signed, Allah revealed the verse: **"O prophet, Surely We [Allah] have granted you a manifest victory [as the treaty of al-Hudaybia]"** (48:1). Allah also named a chapter of the Quran *al-Fath* after the treaty.

When the Prophet[PBUH] informed Umar about the above verse, he was overwhelmed with happiness and deeply regretted his earlier attitude. During the lifetime of the Prophet[PBUH], Muslims had to fight many defensive battles, and many times, they were victorious. However, the Quran does not call any bravely achieved *battlefield triumph a manifest victory*. Only the *peace treaty* is granted such a high status. Does not that make peace, ceasefire, and negotiation more desirable than violence?

Failed Plan to Stop Conversion and Freedom of Abu Jandal

It turned out that Suhayl ibn Amr's plan to prevent conversion to Islam did not work. Despite the signing of the Treaty of Hudaybia, many pagans in Mecca continued to convert. These individuals knew that they could not find refuge among Muslims in Medina. So, the new converts started to move to a place called Saif Al-Bahr. Ultimately, Abu Jandal broke free from captivity for a second time and made his way to Saif Al-Bahr. The treaty of Hudaybia was not binding on this group, so they started to attack the vulnerable pagan caravans and harass them. The Mecca pagans soon realized it was not easy to control the new converts, so they requested the Prophet[PBUH] to disregard the treaty clause related to the extradition of the refugees.[124] Soon after that, the new converts, including Abu Jandal, joined the Muslim community in Medina. Abu Jandal became a close companion of the Prophet[PBUH] and enthusiastically participated in many campaigns with the Prophet[PBUH].

THE ANALYSIS OF THE TREATY OF al-HUDAYBIA

Before the treaty of Hudaybia was signed, Muslims in Medina had lived under constant threat of attack by more powerful pagan armies for nearly six years. The treaty ended the threat. Muslims became free to travel, do business, and preach Islam. Through this treaty, the Prophet[PBUH] also saved a few Muslims from zulm who were still living in Mecca.

The Prophet[PBUH] was probably the first person in history to find a solution to so much hostility *without violence*. He did not propose merely a theoretical concept; he provided a practical example in the Treaty of al-Hudaybia, a cornerstone declaration of coexistence. It demonstrated the power of understanding, diplomacy, and compromise to resolve conflicts peacefully. What a remarkable display of planning, determination, and execution!

The news of the extraordinary and groundbreaking peace treaty spread rapidly. The accord was hailed as a beacon of hope for resolving the long-standing conflicts all over Arabia. For centuries, desert Arabs were adept at combat tactics and strategies for defeating their opponents. They passed down this knowledge through generations till it became a vital part of their culture. However, a skillfully negotiated peace treaty gave them an unusual message: *Islam is a religion of compromise, tolerance, and peace.*

Islam thrives best in a peaceful environment, and within the next two years after the treaty, almost all of Arabia converted to Islam. For example, when the Prophet[PBUH] signed the peace treaty, he had only 1,400 people with him. After about two years, when the pagans of Mecca broke the peace treaty, and the Prophet[PBUH] decided to liberate Mecca, he had 10,000 people with him. By that time, most of the pagans of Mecca had converted to Islam.

Syrian scholar Dr. M S Ramadan Al-Bouti explained three reasons why the Quran calls the treaty a clear [manifest] victory:

"Official Recognition: The Quraysh's willingness to negotiate acknowledged the Muslims as a legitimate force, marking a turning point in their status in Arabia.

Spread of Islam: *The truce allowed for peaceful outreach*, leading to a substantial increase in conversions and support from other tribes.

Strengthening Internal Unity: With peace secured, the Prophet[PBUH] could address internal challenges, reinforcing the community's stability in Medina."[125]

Today, do Muslims still follow the footsteps of Prophet Muhammad[PBUH] and practice similar compromise, tolerance, and peace?

Analysis of Abu Jandal's Character

Abu Jandal's story offers powerful insights into resilience and spiritual strength. His experience reminds us that even in the face of adversity, we have the capacity to find our inner strength and stay true to our beliefs.

Before handing Abu Jandal back to the pagan authority, the Prophet[PBUH] explained the reason: "We have made the pledge in the name of Allah. We are, therefore, under no circumstances prepared to break it." Nonetheless, the Prophet[PBUH] gave him a remarkable piece of guidance: " Be patient, *resign yourself to the Will of Allah*. He is going to provide … relief ."

Is it easy to be patient? Depends on the circumstances. We easily exercise patience when we wait in a car for the traffic light to turn green. What about exercising patience in the following case?

Abu Jandal was innocent and had committed no crime; he simply followed his heart and embraced Islam. Nonetheless, the pagans severely punished him. We have already glimpsed the pagans' brutality in Chapter 2. When Abu Jandal heard about the Muslim pilgrims, he managed to escape from the pagan captivity to seek shelter in the Muslim camp. He had no idea that he was a few minutes late, and the Prophet^PBUH had already made a commitment with the pagans in the name of Allah. Even if it was not his fault, he had to be handed back to the pagans' authority to endure further torture. He had no clue how long his second captivity and torture would last. Every single moment in captivity must have been extremely difficult for him. In addition to his physical suffering, imagine his emotional turmoil when Muslims failed to provide him shelter. He had no idea if he would survive the second phase of pagan captivity. With this background, was it possible for him to be patient?

To answer this question, the following background is necessary. Humans are tested with different challenges. A lot of events happen that we fail to understand. That is because the Quran states, "**Allah knows, but you do not know**" (2:216). The only solution is patience, which is essentially emotional self-control.

The Quran places an overwhelming emphasis on patience, which is a blessing from Allah: "**Be patient, and your patience is not but by (the assistance of) Allah**" (16:127). Allah praises the patient people: "**Exercise patience; God is with those who have patience**" (8:46). The Quran includes numerous prayers that believers can use to nurture patience: "**Our Lord! Pour forth on us patience**" (2:250).

Now, we are in a position to answer the previous question: "Was it possible for Abu Jandal to be patient while facing so many challenges?" The answer is yes, because the Prophet^PBUH provided the solution: "Be patient, *resign yourself to the Will of Allah* [*emotionally accept* whatever happens to you as a decree from Allah]." A person who surrenders to the Will of Allah will *never be afraid of the future because such a person realizes that Allah is the one who shapes the future (both pleasant and unpleasant)*. If Allah selects something for us, it will always be good for our long-term benefit. The Quran also says: "**Allah**

does not impose on any soul a responsibility beyond its ability" (2:286). Emotional Acceptance of unpleasant events triggers the mental healing process. Even if the physical pain remains, such mental acceptance helps to alleviate emotional conflicts, confusion, and negative thoughts. Such a person grows above all kinds of threats, jealousies, fears, anger, worries, or hate. Such people love themselves unconditionally. They are also kind and polite to themselves. They make progress towards *Nafs-e-Mutma'inna*. People who accept the Will of Allah free themselves of all emotional burdens. They are better prepared to act against injustice and seek solutions. The Quran says: **"God is with those who have patience"** (8:46).

What Comes After Patience and Emotional Acceptance?

In Islam, patience does not mean withdrawing from reality or giving up. Instead, believers are required to make an effort using all allowable means to find a solution and protect themselves from zulm. If the first attempt fails, try again and again, perhaps with different strategies. If further attempts are not possible, then what? The believer should then accept the Will of Allah (also see Chapter 2, heading "Protecting Self from Zulm of Others"). Throughout this process, the believer should continue to pray to Allah for relief.

Abu Jandal's story conveys the following lessons:

1. Despite repeatedly enduring torture, he never abandoned his faith in Islam, demonstrating a commendable and unwavering belief in Allah. His story serves as a reminder of the strength of faith and the importance of standing firm in the face of adversity. This exemplifies the true essence of Islam.
2. After being returned to the pagans, as expected in Islam, he kept making efforts and finally escaped the captivity again. He never gave up hope in Allah.
3. After the initial shock, he was not the least bit bitter that Muslims did not give him shelter. He understood that it was the circumstances and that Muslims were not at fault. The proof is that he joined the Prophet[PBUH] in Medina and enthusiastically participated in many campaigns. He truly resigned himself to the Will of Allah and, without any resentment, rose above the unpleasant experiences and memories. He trusted that Allah had a

higher plan for him and that everything would work out in the end. This is an excellent example of spiritual growth.

May Allah bless the Prophet[PBUH], Abu Jandal, and other dedicated Companions for their sacrifices, perseverance, and sincerity.

In Islam, peace and negotiation have higher priority than violence.

CHAPTER 5

ISLAMIC GUIDELINES FOR HANDLING CRISES

*H*ow can we respond to life's major challenges to minimize suffering and accelerate *the healing process?* We can discover valuable insights into crisis management by delving into the life of Prophet Muhammad[PBUH]. This chapter unveils a profound narrative, depicting a day so arduous that the Prophet himself deemed *it the most challenging day of his life.* What did he pray under such pressure? Despite facing demoralizing and seemingly insurmountable circumstances, how did he manage to sustain hope and continue his efforts? When we seek answers to the above questions, we unlock wisdom from his experiences to navigate any crisis in our lives with grace, resilience, and patience.

The Prophet[PBUH] faced this difficult day during his trip to the city of Taif in 620 CE. That was the time when the Prophet[PBUH], along with most Muslims, were living in Mecca and were facing continuous persecution by the pagans (i.e., about two years before he and most Muslims migrated to Medina –Chapter 3).

HOW DID THE PROPHET[PBUH] RESPOND TO A CRISIS SITUATION?

The Prophet belonged to a tribe called *Quraish,* and his uncle Abu Talib was the tribal chief. When the Prophet started preaching Islam, prominent members of the Quraish tribe and leaders of several Arab tribes strongly resented the new religion. However, using the leverage of tribal loyalty, Abu Talib protected the Prophet from most verbal and physical abuse.

The Prophet's Uncle Abu Talib passed away in the tenth year of Prophethood. At that time, the Prophet and most Muslims lived in Mecca, where they were surrounded by overtly dominant and aggressive pagans. The new tribal chief of the Quraish withdrew his tribal support for the Prophet. The prophet, along with other Muslims, faced continuous hardships. Once, the Prophet commented, "By God, the Quraish never

81

harmed me so much as after the death of Abu Talib."[126] With so much hate and animosity, it was difficult to publicly practice Islamic worship rituals and carry out the Prophetic mission of preaching Islam to others. Throughout this ordeal, the Prophet[PBUH] considered various peaceful strategies to protect himself and the Muslims in Mecca from zulm.

He planned for Muslims to migrate to another location where the residents were friendly towards Muslims and where the culture was more or less similar to Meccan culture. However, this plan came with its own set of challenges. For example, the desert region had very limited resources, including water, to be shared with new immigrants.

As a solution, in 615 CE, the Prophet allowed some Muslims to move to Abyssinia (Ethiopia), where they were safe from the hostility of Mecca's pagans. However, the significant difference in cultural environments between Mecca and Ethiopia made large-scale migration unsuitable for most Muslims of that era.

Around 620 CE, the Prophet[PBUH] thought of a plan to move Muslims to the city of Taif, which is about 60 kilometers from Mecca. However, the people of Taif refused to help Muslims. The section below outlines the difficulties the Prophet[PBUH] encountered during his journey to Taif.

Prophet's[PBUH] Trip to Taif

The Prophet[PBUH] traveled to Taif with one companion, Zaid. The success of his plan depended on whether Taif's people would convert to Islam and would agree to accept Muslim migrants from Mecca. Even if the odds were against him, the Prophet took a chance. The Prophet stayed in Taif for ten days to preach Islam to the people and their chieftains. All of them rejected the Prophet in a very rude manner. Later, their verbal abuse turned violent. According to the Indian scholar Saifur Rahman al-Mubarakpuri, "The people hooted him [the Prophet] through the alley-ways, pelted him with stones and obliged him to flee from the city pursued by a relentless rabble. Blood flowed down both his legs, and Zaid, endeavoring to shield him, was wounded in the head. The mob did not desist until they had chased him two or three miles across the sandy plains to the foot of the surrounding hills. There, wearied and exhausted, he took refuge in one of the numerous orchards and rested against the wall of a vineyard."[127]

Let us take a moment to reflect on the several challenges the Prophet[PBUH] faced at that time. His efforts to find a safe refuge in Taif for Muslims failed. Taif residents launched a deadly attack, physically injuring him, and his legs were bleeding. The aggression of Taif's people was likely to bolster the hostile resolve of Mecca's pagans. As a result, it was no longer safe for him to return home to Mecca. It seems that he and the Muslims had no hope left. Later, the Prophet said that it was the most challenging day of his life. In such a desperate moment, while hiding in the vineyard, he prayed:

O Allah! To You alone, I make complaint of my helplessness, the lack of my resources, and my insignificance before mankind. You are the most Merciful of the mercifuls. You are the Lord of the helpless and the weak, O Lord of mine! Into whose hands would You abandon me: into the hands of an unsympathetic distant relative who would sullenly frown at me or to the enemy who has been given control over my affairs? But if Your wrath does not fall on me, there is nothing for me to worry about. I seek protection in the light of Your Countenance, which illuminates the heavens and dispels darkness, and which controls all affairs in this world as well as in the Hereafter. May it never be that I should incur Your wrath, or that You should be wrathful to me. And there is no power nor resource, but Yours alone.[128]

ANALYSIS OF THE PROPHET'S[PBUH] PRAYER

The Islamic concept of God is not the same as God-of-Philosophy

There is an ideological difference between the philosophical interpretation of God and the Islamic concept of God. Philosophers are free thinkers who proudly trample on conventional religious thinking.

Philosophers sometimes *imagine* their own version of God. Next, they scrutinize if their version of God passes the test of human reasoning and logic. If philosophers' God did not measure up to human standards, they would severely criticize God. *Nauzubillah* (it means "we seek refuge from Allah"). For example, the following argument is attributed to the Greek philosopher Epicurus (died 270 BCE)[129]:

Is God willing to prevent evil but not able to?
Then He is not omnipotent.

83

Is he able but not willing? Then, He is malevolent.
Is he both able and willing? Then whence cometh evil?
Is he neither able nor willing? Then why call Him God?

NOTE: If you are interested in finding out the Quranic answers to the above objections, please check the author's book "Skeptic? Simple Answers Using Quran and Science" on Amazon.

Unlike the God-of-philosophy, Muslims are supposed to always praise Allah in the best possible words, like: **"All praise belongs to Allah, Lord of the worlds"** (1:2). If Allah blesses us with prosperity and comfort, then we should thank, praise, and glorify Allah. If we encounter challenges and hardships, it means Allah is testing us, which is *always* intended for our long-term benefit. Sometimes, we do not understand it all because we have limited knowledge. Thus, we honor and praise the compassionate and gracious Allah in all circumstances. This unwavering faith and love of Allah becomes a source of strength and comfort during difficult times.

After facing unexpected aggression from the Taif inhabitants, it seemed there was no hope for the Prophet[PBUH] and Muslims who were facing persecution in Mecca. Under such desperate circumstances, it is noteworthy how the Prophet[PBUH] addressed Allah: "You are the most Merciful of the mercifuls. You are the Lord of the helpless and the weak." Similarly, when the Prophet's[PBUH] infant son died, he prayed, "But we do not say anything except that which please our Lord" (Chapter 1, heading "The Islamic Art of Handling Heartbreak").

The Prophet's[PBUH] prayers show the beauty of the Islamic concept of God – *Muslims must unconditionally love Allah under all circumstances and always praise Him.* Otherwise, love is conditional.

Communicating to Allah about difficult Circumstances

Muslims are expected to praise Allah in all circumstances. This, however, does not mean they cannot communicate with Allah. For example, Muslims are free to complain to Allah about their *challenging circumstances and personal difficulties*. Please recall the prayers by the Prophet[PBUH] Moosa and Zakariyah[PBUH], who complained to Allah about personal challenges

(Chapter 1 heading "Is It Allowed to Use Unconditional Love to Ask for Allah's Favors?"). These prayers not only show that it is allowed to complain to Allah about personal problems but also seek Allah's help to resolve them.

In the context of Taif, the Prophet[PBUH] prayed: "O Lord of mine! Into whose hands would You abandon me: into the hands of an unsympathetic distant relative who would sullenly frown at me or to the enemy who has been given control over my affairs?" Here, the Prophet[PBUH] complained to Allah about *future* threats ("Into whose hands would You abandon me...") and also about the atrocities of relatives and enemies.

Even if the situation was unbearable for the Prophet[PBUH], without criticizing Allah, the Prophet[PBUH] surrendered to the decree of Allah by saying: "If Your wrath does not fall on me, there is nothing for me to worry about." The Prophet[PBUH] praised Allah by saying, "You are the most Merciful of the mercifuls."

Communicating to Allah by Openly Expressing the Emotions

In addition to complaining about various challenges, believers are allowed to express their most intimate emotions to Allah as long as they do not criticize Him. For example, when the Prophet's[PBUH] infant son died, the Prophet[PBUH] cried and prayed, "The eyes send their tears, and the heart is saddened, but we do not say anything except that which pleases our Lord. O Ibrahim, we are grieving your departure."[130]

Some spiritually developed believers become so accustomed to communicating their emotions to Allah that they do not feel the need to share their feelings with other humans. When Prophet Yaqub[PBUH] was desperate because he had lost two sons, he said, "**I only complain about my sorrow and grief to Allah**" (12:86). Here, Prophet Yaqub[PBUH] was more comfortable expressing his emotions to Allah than to other humans.

Building a communicating relationship with Allah is a lifelong journey. It requires sincerity, devotion, humility, and consistent efforts.

The Belief in Allah Remained Unchanged

In desperate moments, some people get angry with their adversaries or with God; they lose all hope or become atheists. But the above prayer shows that the Prophet had unwavering faith and total trust in Allah. The Prophet truly believed that Allah has absolute control over everything. Having such strong faith reduces the emotional suffering from all worldly calamities because the believer remembers that only merciful Allah can make all events occur, and He has justifications beyond human comprehension.

What did the Prophet^{PBUH} __NOT__ pray for?

To appreciate the above prayer, consider what the Prophet did *not* pray for! The Prophet did not curse the pagans of Mecca or the people of Taif (also see Chapter 1, "Islam Teaches Unconditional Love"). Here, we see another example of *unconditional love*.

If a large number of tribe members had attacked an average person, and he narrowly escaped death, then he would have been consumed by anger, hate, and fear. Such a person would have cursed the entire tribe. The following section demonstrates that the Prophet^{PBUH} remained entirely free of hate and anger. How did he develop such a peaceful and calm temperament? Here, we see a beautiful example of *Nafs-e-Mutma'inna* at work, which removes all kinds of negative emotions. Such a person does not have lingering, non-productive anger against *anyone*. As a result, one does not waste energy on planning revenge or holding back unconditional love. Such a person leads a peaceful life, free from negative thoughts and stress. It also allows one to be more empathetic and compassionate towards others.

The Prophet^{PBUH} Even Prayed _for_ The People of Taif

Out of his exemplary compassion and forgiveness, even when facing so much opposition, the Prophet^{PBUH} did not hesitate to pray for the people of Taif. Shortly after reciting the above prayer, instead of expressing hate and anger, the Prophet prayed to Allah, "I do hope that Allah will bring forth from their [people of Taif] progeny those who would worship Allah alone and not associate partners with Him."[131] Allah accepted the Prophet's^{PBUH} prayer, and the second generation of Taif's people became Muslims. Becoming a *good* Muslim means entry to paradise, which is the highest success any human can possibly achieve.

Again, we also get an unmistakable glimpse of Prophet's^{PBUH} unconditional *love for humanity*. This demonstrates the Prophet's genuine dedication to his role as Allah's messenger and spreading Islam among the people. While facing such a challenging ordeal, only a few can maintain such remarkable patience. Similar to the Prophet[PBUH], every Muslim should aspire to have such a profound faith.

The Prophet[PBUH] Remained Hopeful

The Prophet did not lose hope either. He prayed: "I seek protection in the light of Your Countenance, which illuminates the heavens and dispels darkness, and which controls all affairs in this world as well as in the Hereafter." That is because the Quran prohibits hopelessness and despair: **"Never give up hope of Allah's mercy"** (12:87). The Quran encourages us to be patient and trust Allah's plan. It also encourages us to be grateful for our blessings, strive to do good, and have complete faith in Allah's long-term goals.

Practical Illustration: How to acquire the state of God-Consciousness (Taqwa)

Let us analyze the sentence of the Prophet's[PBUH] prayer: "But if Your [Allah] wrath does not fall on me, there is nothing for me to worry about." Even if the Prophet[PBUH] was going through such a difficult phase, and the cumulative problems seemed unsurmountable, the above prayer shows that *he was not overwhelmed by the circumstances.* Instead, *he remained fully focused to avoid Allah's displeasure.* Our primary concern should be to do our best so that Allah blesses us with a good afterlife, which is much more important than the difficulties we face in this world.

When Muslims reach this level of spiritual growth, where their concern is to please Allah, they will no longer willingly sin. This heightened state of awareness is called God-consciousness or *Taqwa*. Persons with *Taqwa* are always mindful of their deeds, ensuring they align with Islamic principles.

Even if the Prophet[PBUH] emotionally accepted the difficulties and challenges, he still *prayed for better circumstances*, "I seek protection in the light of Your Countenance, which illuminates the heavens and dispels darkness, and which controls all affairs in this world as well as in the Hereafter." Emotional acceptance of difficulties does not mean we distance ourselves from Allah. We always depend on Allah's help to find the solution.

The Prophet[PBUH] Prayed <u>Directly</u> to Allah

The above prayer demonstrates that the Prophet[PBUH] prayed directly to Allah. This prayer aligns with the rest of the prayers found in the Quran, which includes numerous supplications; each one is directed exclusively to Allah and no one else. For example, Prophet Moses[PBUH] called for help *directly* from Allah. **"*O Lord*! Surely, I am in desperate need of whatever good You may send down to me"** (28:24).

No prayer in the Quran is made to an angel, intercessor, intermediary, scholar, saint, prophet, or divine being other than Allah. In the above prayer, Prophet Moses[PBUH] did *not* request help from his deceased predecessor, Prophet Abraham[PBUH]. Likewise, Prophet Moses[PBUH] did not ask the soul of Prophet Abraham[PBUH] to pray on his behalf to Allah. Instead, Prophet Moses[PBUH] prayed *directly* to Allah, knowing He is the only one who can grant his requests.

While a believer is *alive*, he or she can pray for others: "**O Allah! Guide *us* to the right way**" (1:6). This verse is a prayer for 'us' which means all humanity. Islam also allows believers to request a *living* person to pray for a justified cause. Regarding worldly tasks (like passing salt or opening a door), Muslims are allowed to seek help from any suitable person. Here, the helping person must be alive, listening, and capable of helping. Why? So that the helper is perceived only as human and not as a divine being. Like the Prophet's[PBUH] above prayer, we can and should also seek Allah's help in worldly affairs. Nonetheless, they should still exert maximum effort to achieve their earthly objectives.

RELENTLESS, CONTINUOUS, AND PERSISTENT EFFORTS

On the way back from Taif, the Prophet[PBUH] and Zaid realized that the incident of the physical attack on the Prophet[PBUH] would embolden the pagans of Mecca. Zaid recalled that the pagans of Mecca had recently expelled the Prophet[PBUH] along with other Muslims from the city of Mecca, where they were pushed to the brink of starvation. Zaid was concerned that after the incident in Taif, the pagans were likely to assassinate the Prophet[PBUH]. But the Prophet[PBUH] remained hopeful and fully trusted Allah's judgment. The Prophet[PBUH] told Zaid, "Allah will surely provide relief, and He will verily support His religion and Prophet."[132] After such a harrowing experience in Taif, only very courageous people can stay hopeful.

The Prophet[PBUH] thought of a strategy to enter Mecca with safety and dignity. The Prophet[PBUH] sent a messenger of the Khuza'ah tribe to a prominent pagan in Mecca, Al-Akhnas bin Shuraiq, and requested his protection. In that era, it was customary for a distinguished person to voluntarily give protection to a needy person from physical attack by others. Al-Akhnas bin Shuraiq turned down the Prophet's proposal because he was an ally of the Quraish. Next, the Prophet sent the same message to another pagan, Suhail bin Amr, who also refused. Without giving up, the Prophet sent the same message to another pagan leader, Al-Mut'im bin 'Adi. He agreed to provide protection. He put together a group of his people who were fully armed to escort the Prophet to Kaba to offer prayer and then to the Prophet's[PBUH] home.[133]

Following this incident, the Prophet continued his efforts and, a couple of years later, successfully established a safe haven for Muslims in the city of Medina. There, Muslims were free to unite and defend themselves against the aggression of pagans, *Alhamdulillah* (all praise is to Allah). When facing a calamity, a Muslim should fear only Allah, pray, trust Allah, have hope in Allah, and practice patience. *At the same time, Muslims are required to make their best efforts to resolve the crisis and protect themselves.*

When we examine the Prophet's[PBUH] efforts, from planning Taif's trip to finding refuge in Mecca, we can appreciate how the Prophet foresaw potential challenges, considered available options, and acted on revised plans. Ultimately, Allah blessed him with the desired outcome.

Setbacks and Failures are Part of Life

Even when the Prophet was carrying out the mission of Allah and the Muslims were being unjustly oppressed, still his every effort was not immediately rewarded. Just like our Prophet[PBUH], when our efforts fail, it is essential for believers not to lose hope. Giving up without making adequate efforts is also not an option. Instead, we should stay positive and view failure as an opportunity to learn.

SUMMARY: HOW TO RESPOND TO LIFE'S CHALLENGES?

Here are the main points:

1. When we confront a crisis, we are overwhelmed with all kinds of negative emotions. So, the first step is to take refuge in Allah from the outcast Satan and pray to Allah to remove all negative emotions (described in the next chapter).
2. Praise Allah.
3. Avoid sin (*Taqwa*). Be patient.
4. Complain to Allah about our difficult circumstances and our emotional state.

5. *Emotionally accept* the challenges that we face. In other words, surrender to Allah's decree.
6. *Pray* to Allah to make it easy for us.
7. Make a full *effort* to resolve the problem.

It is the duty of today's Muslims to follow the example of their Prophet. Muslims should strive to be kind and compassionate and avoid all kinds of zulm. They should be mindful of their actions (*Taqwa*) and strive to leave a legacy of goodness.

Communicate with Allah by openly expressing your emotions feelings and concerns.

CHAPTER 6

STARTING THE JOURNEY OF ISLAMIC SPIRITUALITY

I n Chapter 1, we briefly discussed **"(Fully) contented soul"** (89:27) or *Nafs-e-Mutma'inna*. To understand the context better, let us examine the next verse. "**Return to your Lord, [you are] well-pleased with Him, and He [Allah] is also pleased with you. Enter among My servants into My Paradise**" (89:28-30). When the two verses are read together, we can see that the verse (89:28) describes the traits of the people who have *Nafs-e-Mutma'inna*.

HOW CAN ONE BECOME <u>COMPLETELY</u> PLEASED WITH ALLAH?

Muslims believe that *only* Allah can make all events occur: "**Allah has power over all things**" (65:12). According to verses 89:27 to 89:30, to qualify for Paradise, we should be fully content and at total peace with *whatever* Allah has given us during worldly life. So that we can fulfill the requirement: "**[you are] well-pleased with Him [Allah]**" (89:28). This encompasses all events—even those that caused suffering and went against our desires. For example, the passing away of a loved one. To be *thoroughly contented* with life is not an easy task. Life throws various challenges our way: physical hardships, emotional turmoil, political complexities, social dilemmas, environmental issues, confusion caused by rapidly changing technologies, and existential ponderings.

Emotional Surrender to Commands of Allah and Inner Peace

The previous chapter featured an excellent example of Prophet's[PBUH] emotional resilience in his prayer after the setback in Taif. The Prophet[PBUH] prayed: "But if Your [Allah] wrath does not fall on me, <u>there is nothing for me to worry about</u>." These words demonstrate that all along, the

Prophet's[PBUH] main concern was avoiding Allah's wrath or pleasing Allah. Apart from that, he *wholeheartedly embraced* all past and present events emotionally because he said that if Allah is pleased with him, then "there is nothing for me to worry about." This includes all the suffering caused by the Taif trip. The Prophet[PBUH] believed Allah's decisions were fair and just. He accepted his fate with humility and submission. He fully believed that Allah's plans always have long-term benefits.

We explored in Chapter 1 (heading "The Islamic Art of Handling Heartbreak") that *immediately* after facing distressing events, temporarily, it is permissible to feel negative emotions. However, committed believers are expected to quickly recover and return to a state of inner peace and contentment. Is it humanly possible to maintain such a personality? Yes, *it is possible*. That is what the Prophet[PBUH] did after the Taif setback. After the initial momentary shock, he was able to regain his composure. With this newfound strength, he was able to continue an all-out effort to protect himself and the Muslims in Mecca. He became completely free of hate, fear, and anger. Without any negative emotions bothering him, *he even prayed for the people of Taif.*

Just like the Prophet[PBUH], during calamities, all Muslims are expected to emotionally surrender to whatever Allah sends their way and remain patient and steadfast in their faith. Given this background, it should not be surprising that the word *Islam* means *total submission* to all commands of Allah or whatever Allah gives us. According to Princeton University's *Muslim Life Program* website ISLAMFYI: "The word "Islam" is often literally translated as *submission* ..., the meaning of submission in Islam is not a forceful submission. Rather, it is a peaceful, willing submission where the individual realizes a higher power and submits fully to God's teachings and preferences or will over their own ego and vices. *The vision of Islam is that this coming into harmony with the divine will create an internal and external peace for the soul and for society at large.*"[134] The last sentence has the same concept as the verse: **[you are] well-pleased with Him [Allah], and He is also pleased with you"** (89:28).

Rumi said:

> This being human is a guest house.
> Every morning, a new arrival.

A joy, a depression, a meanness, some momentary awareness comes as an unexpected visitor.

Welcome and entertain them all! Even if they're a crowd of sorrows, who violently sweep your house empty of its furniture, still treat each guest honorably.

He may be clearing you out for some new delight.

The dark thought, the shame, the malice, meet them at the door laughing, and invite them in.

Be grateful for whoever comes, because each has been sent as a guide from beyond.[135]

The path towards *Nafs-e-Mutma'inna* is a lifelong journey where you continually strive for personal growth, piety, and unconditional love. As you make progress, the path becomes smoother and more rewarding. Allah's boundless mercy is there to guide and help you every step of the way. Sufi Inayat Khan said,

When the soul is attuned to God, every action becomes music.[136]

How to Please Allah?

The second half of the above verse (89:28) leads to the question: *what will make Allah please with us?* The Quran responds: **"Those who believe and do good deeds, Allah will make them enter gardens [Paradise] beneath which rivers flow to abide in them forever"** (4:57). To put it differently, to please Allah, we should have correct belief and do good deeds, which include avoiding zulm.

How do you Know Where You Stand in the Ladder of Spiritual Growth?

The above question may seem complicated, but the idea of *Nafs-e-Mutma'inna* offers valuable insight. Here is a question you can ask yourself:

Am I in complete harmony with myself and the world?

If not, there is still inner work to be done. Even if you answer yes, there is always room for improvement by continuing the spiritually evolving journey towards *Nafs-e-Mutma'inna*. As discussed above, *Nafs-e-Mutma'inna* qualifies a person to enter Paradise. So, this question cannot be ignored. The beauty of *Nafs-e-Mutma'inna* lies in its tangibility—*you can actually feel it and evaluate your status.*

ALLAH GUIDES US AND TESTS US

It is mentioned in the Quran that Allah will test us with various challenges in this life: "**Certainly We [Allah] shall test you with something of fear and hunger, and loss of wealth, and lives, and crops, but give glad tidings to the patient**" (2:155). These tests are not easy. Instead, they challenge our faith, patience, adaptability, and resilience. Our skills are challenged in diverse ways. In some situations, we are required to take practical actions. Other types of tests force us to deal with mental challenges. For example, we may be haunted by lingering unpleasant memories of the past.

However, verses 89:27 and 89:28 convey a deeper message that, despite hardships, we are supposed to make spiritual progress and rise above all physical and emotional suffering as we strive for *Nafs-e-Mutma'inna*. This implies that the challenges and predicaments we face are not there just to make us suffer. Instead, under the guidance from the Quran and hadith and we are expected to *learn from the tests and make spiritual progress.* Even amidst life's fluctuations, we should strive to avoid anger, depression, fear, or hate.

Rumi said:

> On what is fear: Non-acceptance of uncertainty. If we accept that uncertainty, it becomes an adventure! [137]

How should we respond to the challenges? The Quran provides a lot of guidance and optimism. For example, here is good news: "**Certainly, after every difficulty, there comes relief**" (94:6). Life may bring us hardships and challenges, but the Quran reassures us that relief and comfort will also come. We should remember this and stay strong and patient through tough times.

Along with various challenges, Allah also gave humans the continuous blessing of hope: "**Never give up the hope of Allah's mercy**" (12:87). Hope keeps a true believer connected to Allah. Believers no longer depend solely on their individual abilities to resolve situations. They know that merciful Allah is looking after them and trust Him to guide them and provide what is best for them. This hope keeps them focused on their goals and inspires them to continue their efforts.

One more good news: **"God does not impose on any soul a responsibility beyond its ability"** (2:286). This verse teaches us that Allah's trials in this life are tailored not to exceed our ability to endure.

For each individual, Allah's tests have a distinct purpose, as explained by the following Hadith: "Amongst My [Allah's] believing-bondsmen [worshipers] are those whose belief will not be improved except by poverty, and if I enrich them, it will be ruined. And there are amongst My believing bondsmen those whose belief will not be improved except by enriching them, and if I impoverish them, it will be ruined."[138]

In summary, Allah's tests have been carefully customized for each individual to benefit them in the long run.

The Quran justifies our challenges: **"You may not like something which, in fact, is for your good and something that you may love, in fact, maybe evil. Allah knows, but you do not know"** (2:216). Since we have limited knowledge, we must trust Allah and rely on His judgment. *Even if we do not understand it all,* Allah is the most merciful and benevolent. When in doubt, the best advice comes from an Urdu couplet:

> Tu dil mein to aata hi, samajh mein nahi aata
> Main jaan gaya bas teri pehchan yahi hai.

> Allah, I can feel You in my heart but fail to understand You
> Finally, I figured out how to recognize You!

STEPS TO FOLLOW FOR AN ISLAMIC SPIRITUAL JOURNEY

Getting Rid of Negative Emotions

In this section, we will overview the methodology Allah has given humankind to achieve emotional stability and peace of mind even in the face of hardships.

At the outset of the Quran, there is a significant declaration: **"There is no doubt that this book is a guide for those who fear Allah [have Taqwa]"** (2:2). To acquire the state of *Nafs-e-Mutma'inna*, we will be using guidance from the Quran and hadith. *When we notice how lovingly and comprehensively the Quran and hadith guide us, we glimpse the beauty of Islam.*

Here is an example of guidance from the Quran: **"If Satan tries to seduce you, seek refuge in Allah** (7:200). How do we detect that Satan is seducing us? The answer to this question is not straightforward because it requires thorough consideration to prevent all instances of Satanic seduction.

Some temptations of Satan are downright evil and can be identified easily—for example, the temptation to rob a bank or scam someone. If a believer experiences such a thought, seeking refuge in Allah is recommended.

However, a close inspection of human behavior reveals that there are many other situations of seduction by Satan. This includes various negative emotions like fear, depression, insecurity, stress, anger, etc., that prevent us from acquiring *Nafs-e-Mutma'inna*. Suppose years ago, you had a best friend who tricked you and borrowed $1000. He never paid you back and later denied borrowing the money. To keep it simple, suppose you are no longer friends, and now you are financially well off. Therefore, $1000 is no longer a big deal for you. Nonetheless, recalling that your closest friend was cunning and deceitful is quite distressing. That memory can occasionally make you depressed, stressed, angry, and bitter. The desire to eliminate negative emotions from your thoughts is natural, as they hinder achieving peace of mind. For comfort and solace, the Islamic solution is to *seek refuge in Allah*, as the above verse (7:200) suggests.

The analysis of verse (7:200) can be summarized in the following four key points:

1. How to Stop Negative Thoughts Without Using Willpower?

Every adult knows that willpower cannot stop negative thoughts. No matter how hard you try to push a thought away using your willpower, it keeps coming back. This is how the human mind functions. If willpower could eliminate negative thoughts, then everyone would be happy and peaceful all the time.

Islam, on the other hand, expects us to get rid of all negative thoughts and achieve the state of *Nafs-e-Mutma'inna*. How can one get rid of negative thoughts when using willpower does not seem to work? We also learned that Islam does not mandate any worship ritual that is extremely difficult or impossible to perform (Chapter 2). How to solve this perplexing paradox?

Instead of mandating *to forcefully remove the negative thoughts* using willpower, verse (7:200) guides us to *seek refuge in Allah*. We should recite *a'oodhu billaahi min al-shaytaan ir-rajeem* [I seek refuge in Allah from the outcast Satan]. These are very powerful words. Please take a moment to appreciate the practicality of the solution offered by the above line. Its beauty lies in its simplicity and how it can be universally practiced. The best part is that *you eliminate negative thoughts without using willpower!* Besides, even a child or a person who lacks intelligence can recite the above line. When you recite the above line, Satan leaves momentarily. But Satan can come right back and seduce you again. You can keep repeating the line as many times as you like. If suffering does not reduce, practice Islamic rituals, *love Allah unconditionally*, refrain from zulm, and continue to seek refuge in Allah, *who you love more than anything else. Feel Allah's unconditional love when you recite this line*. Once again, *Islamic worship rituals are always simple and practical to follow.*

Another relevant verse can also be used: "**Lord, I seek your protection against the strong temptations of the *Shayatin* (devils). And I seek refuge in Thee! O my Lord! from their presence**" (23:97-98).

2. You Are Not Left Alone

Our mental struggles are deeply personal and private issues that are difficult to share with others. When people struggle with mental challenges like depression or stress, they often feel isolated and all alone. In contrast, when a believer seeks refuge in Allah, then the believer is *definitely not alone*. Besides, nothing can be hidden from Allah. He loves us. He knows all our shortcomings, doubts, abilities, and efforts. By seeking refuge in Allah, the believer feels protected and reassured. This makes a big difference. With this understanding, we are ready to start our journey toward *Nafs-e-Mutma'inna*. All we have to do is identify various situations in which we should seek refuge in Allah.

3. No Self-Analysis is Necessary

You do not need to analyze and identify the guilty party. Such overthinking is usually counter-productive and may complicate the situation. All you need to do is seek refuge in Allah, who knows it all and controls everything. He can solve all problems.

However, sometimes, it is necessary to logically analyze a situation to understand its cause and find a solution. This process becomes significantly easier when you feel Allah is on your side.

Here is the good news: *Even when you have no idea why you feel uneasy or stressed, you can still seek refuge in Allah and love Allah unconditionally.*

4. Relief Begins *Immediately* – Have *Tawakkul* (Trust) in Allah

Islamic understanding of God fosters a positive and balanced mindset. It emphasizes the oneness and uniqueness of Allah, encouraging believers to develop a sense of accountability, compassion, and purpose in their lives. Simultaneously, Allah is close to believers because He is the most merciful, most benevolent, most wise, most loving, most just, most forgiving, and most caring. He always guides us toward our long-term benefit. Believers embrace with their hearts whatever Allah has ordained for them in the past, their current circumstances, and what lies ahead. This acceptance leads them to relinquish the false belief that they can control the world through sheer willpower or meticulous planning. Such emotional surrender or *Tawakkul* gives immense relief and peace. *Tawakkul* refers to having faith in Allah, trusting that He will provide what is best for you. However, *Tawakkul* requires nurturing and persistent effort over time. It is the gateway to *Nafs-e-Mutma'inna*.

After the harrowing Taif setback, when the Prophet[PBUH] was resting in the vineyard, he realized that despite his best efforts, his plan to protect Muslims in Mecca by moving them to Taif had failed. An ordinary person would have been disappointed to the point of getting lost. Instead, we can see *Tawakkul* in the Prophet's[PBUH] prayer, "There is no power nor resource, but Yours alone." To put it differently, the Prophet[PBUH] completely relied only on Allah for help, guidance, and solutions. *Tawakkul* can remove all kinds of negative emotions. No wonder, shortly after the Taif incident, the Prophet[PBUH] *prayed* for the progeny of the people of Taif. Only a person who does not have even a trace of fear, anger, hate, or a desire to take revenge can do that.

The Quran makes *Tawakkul* an integral part of the Islamic faith:

"Have *Tawakkul* in God if you are true believers" (5:23).

"God is sufficient for the needs of whoever has *Tawakkul* in Him"
(65:3).

"Moses told his people, "If you have submitted yourselves to God
and have faith in Him, have *Tawakkul* in Him" (10:84).

If you have Tawakkul, why make an effort?

If God controls everything, it raises the fundamental question: if the sole
determining factor is the will of God, why should humans strive for
anything at all? Does *Tawakkul* mean human efforts have no meaning?
Without getting into the complexities of the Omnipotence Paradox, about
1400 years ago, an Arab asked the Prophet[PBUH] this question in very simple
language: "Shall I tie it (my camel) and rely (upon Allah to protect it), or
leave it loose and rely (upon Allah to protect it)?" The Prophet[PBUH]
responded, "*Tie* the camel and then *rely (upon Allah).*"

The above hadith tells us that *Tawakkul* upon Allah not only coexists with
making a full effort, but in some cases, making an effort is a requirement.
For example, tying the camel.

> In Islam, *Tawakkul* coexists with making an effort. However, humans
> have limited understanding (2:216) and cannot fully grasp this concept.

Power of Dhikr (Remembering Allah)

A crucial question still needs an answer: *How can humans experience almost
continuous happiness, peace, and contention?* The Quran provides the answer:
"**Remembrance [Arabic word Dhikr used here] of Allah <u>certainly</u>
brings comfort to all hearts**" (13:28). The word *Dhikr* means
'remembering Allah.' When we pray the five ritual supplications or recite
any verse of the Quran, we do the dhikr of Allah.

Dhikr encompasses more than just remembering. According to the Muslim
scholar Zainub Habib, "Dhikr is an all-embracing term that, in addition to
including the ritual acts of worship, covers an array of activities of the
tongue and heart. It involves thinking of and making mention of Allah at
all times and in every area of our lives. This is the worship that has no
special time but is performed constantly so that it permanently links up
man's life with Allah and His service.... Ablution is not a prerequisite for
dhikr, and dhikr can be pronounced with the tongue or done silently.

However, when one is saying it, one must not do it with a careless and inattentive heart and try to be conscious of what one is saying."[139]

Habib suggested different ways to do dhikr: "When we glorify Allah by saying *Subhanallah* (How perfect is Allah), when we praise Him by saying *Alhamdulillah* (All praise is for Allah), when we magnify Him by saying *Allahu Akbar* (Allah is the Greatest), all this is dhikr. When we say *Astaghfirullah* (I seek Allah's forgiveness), when we say *La hawla wa la quwwata illa billah* (There is no power nor might except with Allah), all this is dhikr. Our Prophet (saw) also said: "(There are) Two words, (which are) light on the tongue, heavy on the Scale and beloved to The Most Gracious: "*SubhaanAllaahi wa bihamdihi. Subhaan Allaahil azeem.*" (How perfect Allah is and I praise Him. How perfect Allah is, The Supreme)."[140]

The Quran praises the believers as: **"Men who remember Allah standing, sitting and lying down on their sides and contemplate the (wonders of) creation ..."** (3:191). This verse also tells us another method to remember Allah: contemplating His miracles in the universe.

By doing Dhikr, a believer feels closeness to Allah and makes spiritual progress. Engaging in Dhikr is an excellent strategy for replacing irrelevant, random, non-productive thoughts. Thus, Dhikr helps reduce stress and anxiety, improve focus, and increase mindfulness. According to early Egyptian Muslim mystic and ascetic Dhû-l-Nûn:

> I make abundant remembrance of You [Allah] not because I have
> forgotten You; That is simply what flows from the tongue.[141]

Sufi Rabia described dhikr as:
> [Allah] Your hope in my heart is the rarest treasure
> Your Name on my tongue is the sweetest word
> My choicest hours
> Are the hours I spend with You -
> O God, I can't live in this world
> Without remembering You[142]

Unconditional Love Makes All the Difference

Loving Allah unconditionally is a soothing and comforting feeling that makes us aware there is more to life than we experience as isolated, lonely, and struggling individuals. Unconditional love provides strength and support even during catastrophes and the most difficult moments.

During times of crisis, one may feel overwhelmed and lost. That is precisely the time when the power of love for Allah can provide guidance and support. Remember that one is supposed to love Allah *unconditionally*; therefore, just because one is going through a crisis is no excuse to hold back the love of Allah. Turn to Him with wholehearted devotion and find the strength to face any challenge with courage and grace. Trust in His plans, and let your heart be filled with peace. Tell Allah you unconditionally love Him and recite the verse **"The strongest of the believers' love is their love of Allah"** (2:165). Optionally, you may also recite *a'oodhu billaahi min al-shaytaan ir-rajeem* or verses like (3:160) to dispel negative feelings.

However, successfully doing this during a crisis requires practice and dedication. One should also love Allah and feel His love during mundane and calm moments.
Rumi said:

> Something opens our wings.
> Something makes boredom and hurt disappear.
> Someone fills the cup in front of us.
> We taste only sacredness.[143]

More Guidance from the Quran

The Quran has many prayers to help the believers. Those prayers can be used with or without reciting *a'oodhu billaahi min al-shaytaan ir-rajeem*. Only four examples are quoted here:

Prayer for patience: **"Lord, grant us patience"** (7:126).

Prayer for more knowledge: **"My Lord, grant me more knowledge"** (20:114).

Prayer for forgiveness: **"Lord, I have wronged myself. Forgive me!"** (28:16).

Always have Hope in Allah: **"Never give up hope of Allah's mercy"** (12:87).

Example of Controlling the Negative Emotions

Here is an example of Islamic mental control over negative emotions. Immediately after the battle of Uhud, when the Prophet[PBUH] returned to Medina along with the Muslim volunteer army, he heard the news that the pagans, instead of retreating to Mecca, have turned around to attack Medina. They planned to annihilate Muslims.

Even if Muslims were tired and many of them were wounded, the Prophet[PBUH] put together a volunteer Muslim army and marched towards the approaching pagans. When Muslims reached a location called Hamra al-Asad, they received another message that the pagans had assembled a much larger force, and they were all set to invade Madinah and eliminate its people.[144]

Let us try to imagine the negative emotions that a regular person might have experienced. To start with, Muslims must have been physically exhausted after fighting the battle of Uhud and traveling back to Medina. Many Muslims were wounded. Even the Prophet[PBUH] himself was seriously injured. Many were grieving because their friends and relatives were martyred in the battle. Hypocrite Abdullah bin Ubai and his 300 followers betrayed the Muslims right before the battle. Under such circumstances, most people would have felt deceived and defeated. It must have been very demoralizing to realize that the outcome of the battle of Uhad was not in their favor. At that moment, they had no way of knowing if Muslims would ever recover from the losses at Uhud.

When Muslims heard that the reinforced pagan army was marching towards Hamra al-Asad, their morale and willingness to defend Islam increased. Here, we are not just talking about redirecting thoughts, which offer only temporary or partial relief. Instead, *believers completely eliminated all their negative emotions.* This remarkable accomplishment empowers individuals to master their emotions, leading to a more fulfilling life free from worries, anger, threats, and fear. With calm minds, they can handle challenging situations more effectively.

Muslims stood resolutely, prepared to defend themselves. Allah praised the reaction of the Muslims: **"The righteous and pious of those who have pledged obedience to God and the Messenger, after injury had befallen them, will receive a great reward. Such people, when warned to fear those who are gathered against them, are strengthened in their faith, and say, 'God is All-sufficient as our Guardian' "** (3:172, 3:173).

Later, the pagan army got frightened and retreated without fighting Muslims.

The verse (3:173) offers the following valuable insights:

Applicable to All Past, Present, and Future Issues

To remove negative emotions, as the above verse suggests, we can pray: **'God is All-sufficient as our Guardian'** (3:173). This prayer can be used not just on a battlefield but in *every single* challenging situation in our lives. In addition, we can also use this prayer to let go of *past* self-criticism, regrets, and painful recollections of wrongs committed by others. We can also use the same prayer to deal with any *current* predicament. Like the Prophet[PBUH] and companions, we can also use the same prayer to eliminate all our *future* threats and fears.

Thus, just one prayer can remove *all* our past ugly memories, present concerns, and future threats.

Irrespective of the Situation, Benevolent Allah is in Control

Another benefit of this verse was that the believers did not fear the pagans even if they outnumbered them and were very aggressive. Why? Those Muslims believed the most merciful Allah was in total control of every event. Absolutely no event can occur unless the benevolent Allah permits it. Even if an event occurs that is against Muslims' expectations, they will also emotionally accept that unpleasant outcome. This belief brings them peace and freedom from anxiety, knowing that whatever happens is part of Allah's divine plan and is ultimately for their own good. They became peaceful inside and did not waste energy on hatred, fear, or anger. Such a believer *completely surrenders to Allah*. The ability to emotionally accept, with patience and gratitude, all past, present, and future events as part of God's plan is *Tawakul*.

A Good News for the Victim of Zulm

Humans can become victims of all kinds of zulm. Chapter 2 presents only a very narrow subset of various possibilities. Many times, the resulting emotional wounds can last for decades. To demonstrate our strategy, let us think back to the time when your best friend deceived you out of $1000. Every time you recall this incident, you are bombarded with disturbing questions: "Why are some people so cruel?" or "Why was I so gullible?" or "Can I ever trust anyone again?" Such questions seem endless and come in many variations. It is difficult to eliminate these thoughts because, emotionally, it is nearly impossible to ignore the gross injustice. You know these thoughts have been tormenting you for years, and all previous attempts to eliminate them have failed. So, the only option seems to be to put up with the suffering. You may also feel completely *alone*.

Thankfully, the verse "**God is All-sufficient as our Guardian**" (3:173) offers a powerful tool. By repeatedly reciting this verse, you can confront those nagging questions while basking in the unconditional love of Allah. The very first thing you realize is that you are not alone. The omnipotent Allah is by your side, a benevolent guardian and protector, strengthening your faith and guiding you on a spiritual journey.

The Quran tells us that life is a test, and our duty is to grow above suffering and acquire *Nafs-e-Mutma'inna*. When reciting the verse (3:173), recall that the Quran says human knowledge is limited and only Allah has total knowledge. In the long run, a $1000 loss could ultimately benefit you by teaching you how to manage negative emotions. You can repeatedly use the same strategy in any unpleasant situation that creates negative emotions.

Repeatedly reciting the verse (3:173) creates a multitude of conscious and subconscious positive messages. It reinforces our faith and gradually erodes decades-old negative mental habits. One may have to repeatedly recite the verse till the positive messages sink in. This realization makes the entire process enjoyable as you triumph over deep-rooted negative thoughts. Not only that, you are making significant spiritual strides. From that point of view, you were definitely not a *loser*. Ultimately, you will find it possible to emotionally accept the injustice caused by your best friend, allowing you to reclaim your peace of mind. Victims of all kinds of zulm can use this strategy.

INITIAL FEW STEPS TOWARDS ISLAMIC SPIRITUAL GROWTH

Let us talk about an imaginary character named Zahid, who was bullied in school. To keep our discussion simple, let us assume that he is now well-settled as an adult with a family.

However, he continues to grapple with emotional challenges due to years-old memories of being bullied and lingering feelings of humiliation and threat. For decades, Zahid has been trying to push away those painful thoughts using distractions (like going to a friend's party), willpower, and determination, but the uncomfortable thoughts keep coming back.

This helplessness compounds the problem. Sporadically, Zaid finds himself caught in the mental trap of wondering what he could have done differently *in the past* to protect himself from those bullies. Additionally, adult Zahid blames himself for failing to stop the bullies in the *past*.

Eventually, Zahid turned to the Quran for a solution. He learned that the first step towards spiritual growth is an unwavering belief in pure Islamic monotheism (the first pillar of Islam). This belief is reinforced by unconditionally loving Allah and continuously seeking His help and guidance. Under the guidance from the Quran, Zahid revised his strategy.

Every time those painful memories resurface, Zahid recites *a'oodhu billaahi min al-shaytaan ir-rajeem* to seek refuge in Allah from the outcast Satan or verse (23:97-98). These words are not recited without emotions. Instead, Zahid recited while *feeling unconditional love for Allah*, the only one who can protect Zahid. Seeking refuge in Allah is a declaration of entrusting one's worries to a higher power, believing that problems will be resolved entirely. Zahid can also recite the verse, **"God is All-sufficient as our Guardian"** (3:173), with the unconditional love of Allah. This reminds Zahid that whatever happened was Allah's command to test Zahid, and Allah has justification beyond human understanding. Zahid learns to fully trust Allah by reciting (3:160) and prays for patience (7:126) (See list of verses below). To love Allah, Zahid can recite verses (2:165) or (85:14). These two verses also teach Zahid how he can unconditionally love *himself*. That stops all forms of self-blame. Zahid no longer feels the urge to rewind time and protect himself. Unconditional love makes a tremendous difference. It instantaneously gives the feeling of *victory over* negative thoughts. If the negative thoughts come back, seek Allah's refuge again and love Allah unconditionally. Based on the emotional needs of the moment, Zahid can also recite any relevant verse of the Quran, including the following:

> **"God is All-sufficient as our Guardian"** (3:173).
> **"Lord, grant us patience"** (7:126).
> **"Never give up hope of Allah's mercy"** (12:87)

"The strongest of the believers' love is their love of Allah"
(2:165).
"He [Allah] is the All-forgiving, the Most Loving One" (85:14).
"Lord, I have wronged myself. Forgive me!" (28:16).
"O Lord! Surely, I am in desperate need of whatever good that
You may send down to me" (28:24).
"My prayer, sacrifice, life, and death are all for God, the Lord
of the worlds"(6:162).
"The true believers trust in God" (3:160).

When to recite which verse is not a fixed rule because we all have different challenges and are at various levels of spiritual growth. If you are uncertain which verse to choose, seek guidance from Allah to help you choose a suitable verse.

Emotional Surrender Does Not Rule Out Making an Effort

Let us consider another example: if Zahid's car breaks down on the road, he might initially feel distressed. In that case, he may start reciting verses (3:173), (2:165), or (85:14). As his worries and stress become more manageable, he will be in a better position to make sound decisions and take practical steps to resolve the issue of his car breakdown.

The above strategy applies to *every single* emotional challenge throughout life. For example, if Zahid is diagnosed with a terminal disease, and his doctor predicts that he only has two more months to live. Even when Zahid is so close to death, his *inner self* may remain peaceful and content while he continues to thank Allah for all His blessings.

Controlling Emotions in Our Daily Life

Let us consider a small-scale application of the above strategies that can be helpful in the present day. Suppose you studied for several months in preparation for a qualifying exam for a job you desperately need. On the night before the exam, you would like to have a peaceful sleep so you are well-rested and relaxed during the exam. Otherwise, during the exam, you will be unable to use your full potential. You try to lull yourself to sleep, but some thoughts keep bothering you. "What will I do if I fail?" "What if I forget what I have studied?" "I have always failed in everything." One of life's challenges is having to deal with uncertainty when you worry about controlling the outcome of a situation.

107

The only way to block these thoughts and have peaceful sleep is to *emotionally accept whatever is going to happen*. In other words, even if you fail the exam, you will emotionally accept that as a decree of Allah and go on with your life. You may like to repeatedly recite, **'God is All-sufficient as our Guardian'** (3:173) *while loving Allah unconditionally*. Thus, you reassure yourself that Allah's mercy is boundless and He has complete control over every event. His decisions are always meant for our long-term benefit, even if they do not align with our desires. Allah is the best protector and guardian.

Such emotional acceptance will block all non-productive thoughts, allowing you to sleep peacefully. In the morning, you will be able to approach the day with a fresh perspective. Emotionally accepting everything literally means surrendering to the Will of Allah, which is the definition of the word Islam.

Five Pillars of Islam

The Quran says, **"The strongest of the believers' love is their love of Allah"** (2:165). To have *maximum love for Allah*, we should be among the *strongest believers*. To become such a committed believer, one must follow the basic traditions and teachings of Islam, including the following:

(1) Correct monotheism belief in Allah (*Shahada*).
(2) Ritual supplication (*Salat*).
(3) Charity (*Zakat*).
(4) Fasting (*Sawm*).
(5) Hajj Pilgrimage.

When it comes to practicing rituals, not everyone is on the same page. Some regularly pray ritual prayers five times a day, and some do not pray at all. Therefore, regardless of our standpoint, it is crucial to take just one additional step at a time toward meeting the requirement. This will ensure that practicing the rituals remains easy and consistent while we make steady progress in sha Allah (if Allah is willing). The Prophet[PBUH] said, "Religion is very easy, and whoever overburdens himself in his religion will not be able to continue in that way."[145] Similarly, we discussed earlier that rituals should be followed without committing zulm-on-self (Chapter 2, heading "Keeping Religious Rituals Easy and Practical"). The Quran says, **"Allah** intends for your ease, and He does not want to make things difficult for you" (2:185).

Summary

When you learn to love Allah unconditionally and feel His love, you become closer to Allah, and He becomes your best friend. You feel His presence and guidance in everything you do. Your heart is filled with peace and contentment. You learn the art of emotionally accepting whatever Allah sends your way. This helps you to cope with difficult situations and to create a positive outlook. From then on, the first milestone is when you conquer a negative emotion that has troubled you for years. You realize that, in the same manner, you can overpower all other negative emotions.

As you progress on your spiritual journey towards *Nafs-e-Mutma'inna*, you may encounter moments of confusion or feelings of loss. But if you patiently persist and use the strategies described in this book, you will soon find a way out with Allah's help. This journey of unconditional love and spiritual growth gives you peace and tranquility from the moment you start it and lasts throughout your lifetime. Rumi said:

The hurt you embrace becomes joy.[146]

Seeking inner peace by overpowering negative emotions is not an obsolete or impossible perception. Many modern-day scholars also promote the same concept. For example, Puerto Rican poet Denice Frohman puts it beautifully:

> Your wound is probably not your fault, but your healing is your responsibility.[147]

DO YOU PLAN TO ACHIEVE THE STATE OF *NAFS-E-MUTMA'INNA*?

According to the Quran, those with a *Nafs-e-Mutma'inna* will be granted a place in Paradise. That is not all. In this life, *Nafs-e-Mutma'inna* gives us deep serenity, satisfaction, and harmony, allowing us to lead a life of purpose and joy. As guided by the above prayers and rituals, are you willing to take the first step toward experiencing that feeling? Realistically speaking, this is not an easy goal because it involves having to change your habitual ways of thinking. Our mental habits have been with us for almost all our lives.

Whether our mental habits are good or bad, we have somehow learned to live with them. Modifying them can be an arduous undertaking.

Why not give it a try, even if you are hesitant? You might surprise yourself with the results.

Rumi said:

When will you begin that long journey into yourself?[148]

IF YOU ANSWERED **YES** TO *NAFS-E-MUTMA'INNA*

Allah is with you. Allah is your guide and helper. It is immensely inspirational and reassuring to realize that you are not alone. In addition, the Quran tells us to trust Allah and never give up hope. Allah loves us and never burdens us with more than we can handle. Ibn Qayyim Al-Jawziyya said,

Be to Allah as He wishes, and He will be to you more than you can wish for.[149]

IF YOUR ANSWER IS **NO** TO *NAFS-E-MUTMA'INNA*

If you think that achieving *Nafs-e-Mutma'inna* is too demanding and you decide *not* to pursue it, consider this question:

Did you ask for Allah's help?

Otherwise, on the Day of Judgment, what will be your justification for not even trying?

It does not make sense to quit without asking for Allah's help. Success requires only honest intentions, effort, and dedication. **'God is All-sufficient as our Guardian'** (3:173). *Leave the result to Allah.* You will receive Allah's continuous help, in sha Allah.

You have the power to control your negative emotions

Recommended Reading

A portion of this book consists of excerpts from the author's previous book. *The Purest Monotheism: Monotheistic Islam. Polytheistic Muslims,* which was written after 19 years of rigorous study and introspection (Appendix-A). That book, however, contained too much information in condensed form, and many readers found it difficult to absorb. Based on their feedback, the author split his previous book into three digestible segments and published them as independent books with the following titles.

Chapters 1, 2, 5, and 8: *The Greatest Miracle of the Quran: Islamic Monotheism*

Chapters 6 and 7: *ISLAM: Path of Infinite Love*

Chapters 7, 9 to 13: An *Islam Inspired Solution to Radicalism: A Peaceful and Practical Approach*

A NOTE FROM THE AUTHOR

Hopefully, this message finds you savoring Allah's unconditional love. May Allah fill your heart with everlasting love as you embark on your spiritual journey.

Please share your thoughts about my book by writing a review. Your perspective, insights, and reactions are essential in shaping the journey for future readers and for me to grow as a writer.

Writing a review does not require a literary masterpiece. A few sentences expressing what you loved, what stayed with you, or how the book made you feel can make all the difference.

Here is a link to Amazon's book page:
https://www.amazon.com/dp/B07RZH7MYS.
Thanks for your support and feedback.

With sincere appreciation,
Eeshat Ansari

Those who are able to see beyond the shadows and lies of their culture will never be understood, let alone believed by the masses[148]

~ PLATO

APPENDIX A

If you agree with the following message, please email or print this message and share it with Muslim scholars.

From the book *ISLAM: Path of Infinite Love by Dr. Eeshat Ansari*

AN IMPORTANT MESSAGE FOR MUSLIM SCHOLARS

The Quran says: **"Allah does not love those who do *zulm*"** (3:57). Allah emphasizes the concept of justice because the word ع د ل (justice) appears 18 times in the Quran. Similarly, Allah strongly discourages zulm or ظ ل م (injustice, oppression, putting a thing in a place not its own). The Quran references the word *zulm* an impressive 288 times to discourage it (excluding the occurrences of the same root word meaning darkness).

The word *zulm* appears in the following verses. *Only* the verses that use these words in the above meanings are included below. If the word *zulm* appears more than once in a verse, then the verse number is repeated.

Question 1: Have you spoken about *zulm* against women? For example, honor killing, child marriage, female genital mutilation, bride kidnapping (in Kyrgyzstan), wife beating, acid attacks, the imprisonment of rape victims, forced veiling, and restraining women from acquiring education and employment? If not, is this because the above actions are not *zulm,* or because you believe there is a justification for the above actions that has higher priority than avoiding *zulm*?

Question 2: The Quran says that **"Allah wills no injustice [word *zulm* is used here] for (His) slaves"** (40:31). Allah said to Prophet Muhammad[PBUH]: **"We have sent you for no other reason but to be mercy for humankind"** (21:107). If Allah and Prophet Muhammad[PBUH] can only do justice, *is any Muslim scholar allowed to write an exegesis of the Quran or issue a fatwa that leads to injustice and zulm?*

Please Guide Muslims:

- The Quran says: **"You shall not follow anyone *blindly*"** (17:36). Once, an elderly woman openly objected to a new decree from Caliph

114

Umar. He listened to her argument and revised his decree. Similarly, today, if any scholar writes an exegesis of the Quran or gives a fatwa that could lead to *zulm,* then *Muslims have the right to reject such an exegesis or fatwa.*

- Using the above word-count argument, please *repeatedly* guide all Muslims to abstain from corruption, cheating, lying, deceiving, exploiting, scamming, or hurting *anyone* because that is *zulm. By avoiding zulm and practicing justice, Muslims will obey the command of Allah, as emphasized in the following 306 verses of the Quran. As a result, Muslims will re-learn an essential part of Islam that many have forgotten.*

Verses that encourage ʿayn dāl lām (Justice)

4:3, 4:129, 5:8, 5:8, 6:152, 7:159, 7:181, 42:15, 2:282, 2:282, 4:58, 5:95, 5:106, 6:115, 16:76, 16:90, 49:9, and 65:2.

Verses that discourage ẓā lām mīm (oppression):

2:54, 2:57, 2:57, 2:59, 2:59, 2:150, 2:165, 2:231, 2:272, 2:279, 2:279, 2:281, 3:25, 3:117, 3:117, 3:117, 3:135, 3:161, 4:40, 4:49, 4:64, 4:77, 4:110, 4:124, 4:148, 4:168, 6:45, 6:160, 7:9, 7:23, 7:103, 7:160, 7:160, 7:162, 7:162, 7:165, 7:177, 8:25, 8:60, 9:36, 9:70, 9:70, 10:13, 10:44, 10:44, 10:47, 10:52, 10:54, 10:54, 11:37, 11:67, 11:94, 11:101, 11:101, 11:113, 11:116, 14:44, 14:45, 16:33, 16:33, 16:41, 16:85, 16:111, 16:118, 16:118, 17:59, 17:71, 18:49, 18:59, 18:87, 19:60, 21:3, 21:47, 22:39, 23:27, 23:62, 25:19, 26:227, 26:227, 27:11, 27:44, 27:52, 27:85, 28:16, 29:40, 29:40, 29:46, 30:9, 30:9, 30:29, 30:57, 34:19, 34:42, 36:54, 37:22, 38:24, 39:47, 39:51, 39:69, 42:42, 43:39, 43:65, 43:76, 43:76, 45:22, 46:12, 46:19, 51:59, 52:47, 65:1, 4:97, 16:28, 2:114, 2:140, 6:21, 6:93, 6:144, 6:157, 7:37, 10:17, 11:18, 18:15, 18:57, 29:68, 32:22, 39:32, 53:52, 61:7, 4:97, 16:28, 3:182, 8:51, 22:10, 41:46, 50:29, 3:108, 4:10, 4:30, 4:153, 4:160, 5:39, 6:82, 6:131, 11:117, 13:6, 16:61, 20:111, 20:112, 22:25, 25:4, 27:14, 31:13, 40:17, 40:31, 42:41, 14:34, 33:72, 2:35, 2:51, 2:92, 2:95, 2:124, 2:145, 2:193, 2:229, 2:246, 2:254, 2:270, 3:57, 3:94, 3:128, 3:140, 3:151, 3:192, 5:29, 5:45, 5:72, 5:107, 6:21, 6:33, 6:52, 6:58, 6:93, 6:129, 6:135, 7:5, 7:19, 7:41, 7:44, 7:148, 8:54, 9:23, 9:47, 10:39, 10:106, 11:18, 11:31, 11:83, 12:23, 12:75, 12:79, 14:13, 14:22, 14:27, 14:42, 15:78, 16:113, 17:47, 17:82, 17:99, 18:29, 18:35, 18:50, 19:38, 19:72, 21:14, 21:29, 21:46, 21:59, 21:64, 21:87, 21:97, 22:53, 22:71, 23:107, 24:50, 25:8, 25:27, 25:37, 26:209, 28:37, 28:40, 28:59, 29:14, 29:31, 29:49, 31:11, 34:31, 35:32, 35:37, 35:4, 37:63, 37:113, 39:24, 40:18, 40:52, 42:8, 42:21, 42:22, 42:40, 42:44, 42:45, 43:76, 45:19, 49:11, 59:17, 60:9, 62:7, 68:29, 71:24, 71:28, 76:31, 2:258, 3:86, 4:75, 5:51, 6:47, 6:68, 6:144, 7:47, 7:150, 9:19, 9:109, 10:85, 11:44, 23:28, 23:41, 23:94, 26:1, 28:21, 28:25, 28:50, 46:1, 61:7, 62:5, 66:11, 11:102, 21:11, 22:45, 22:48, and 17:33

THE PUREST MONOTHEISM

Monotheistic Islam. Polytheistic Muslims*

by

Dr. Eeshat Ansari

Wisdom, Justice, and Unconditional Love …
These days, Muslims are facing all kinds of problems: persecution by different governments, violence among Muslim sects, women's suppression, mass migration, and more. *Many Muslims have contradictory behavior: they reject modern industrialization and education but depend on modern conveniences.* Even the purity of Islamic monotheism itself is at stake.

Guided by the wisdom of the Quran, this book defines many contemporary problems Muslims face and provides solutions. For example, the Quran strongly condemns zulm (oppression) and uses the word zulm a whopping 288 times to discourage it. So, on what grounds can any Muslim support various oppressions, like preventing women from acquiring education and employment? This book also discusses:
(1) How to *peacefully* end radical Islamic violence.
(2) How Muslim men and women can ideologically respond to oppression by fellow Muslims.
(3) How to bring peace between Muslim sects.
(4) Without calling anyone kafir, how to peacefully preserve the purity of Islamic monotheism.

Sufi literature, accumulated over centuries, proves that loving Allah is the most satisfying spiritual experience. The book describes how to unconditionally love Allah and how to unconditionally love yourself.

Islam places an overwhelming emphasis on love and justice. Prophet Muhammad (PBUH) achieved the first major peaceful transfer of power in history when he took over as the head of state of Medina, even though it was a multi-religious society. On another occasion, instead of waging violent jihad, he proposed the Treaty of al-Hudaybia and made peace with the opponents.

The unique concept of Islamic monotheism also solves philosophical puzzles like the free will-predestination paradox and the watchmaker analogy.

Avalable at: www.amazon.com/dp/B079KDYGH5

* All Muslims are not polytheists. It is inspired by verses 12:106 and the hadith of 73 sects.

NOTES

1 Seeker, D. (n.d.). 50+ Sufi Quotes That Will Inspire and Enlighten Your Sou. Retrieved from Nirvanic: https://nirvanic.co/sufism-quotes/

2 The Invocation of God. Ibn Qayyim al-Jawziyya al-Jawziyya. Translator: M. Abdurrahman Fitzgerald. The invocation of God by page 49. Cambridge. Islamic Texts Society. 2000. 0946621780.

3 Fadiman and Frager. Essential of Sufism. page 119. New York. HarperCollins. 1997. 0785809066.

4 Evans, E. (2024, 2 29). 411 Rumi Quotes to Celebrate Life and Bring Contentment. Retrieved from Brightdrops: https://brightdrops.com/rumi-quotes

5 Ibid.

6 Hamilton, D. D. (2014, 03 14). Why Children Need Love to Grow. Retrieved from drdavidhamilton.com/: https://drdavidhamilton.com/why-children-need-love-to-grow/

7 Britannica. (n.d.). George Sand. Retrieved from Encyclopædia Britannica, Inc.: https://www.britannica.com/quotes/George-Sand

8 Vaughan-Lee, Llewellyn. Travelling the Path of Love: Sayings of Sufi Masters (p. 89). The Golden Sufi Center. Kindle Edition.

9 Evans, E. (2024, 2 29). 411 Rumi Quotes to Celebrate Life and Bring Contentment. Retrieved from Brightdrops: https://brightdrops.com/rumi-quotes

10 Rabia Poems » Reality. (2024, 7 18). Retrieved from Poet Seers: https://www.poetseers.org/spiritual-and-devotional-poets/sufi-poets/rabia-poems/reality.

11 Izzo, John. The Five Thieves of Happiness. s.l. : Berrett-Koehler Publishers, 2017. p. 6.

12 Seeker, D. (n.d.). 50+ Sufi Quotes That Will Inspire and Enlighten Your Sou. Retrieved from Nirvanic: nirvanic.co/sufism-quotes/

13 Ikrimah ibn Abi Jahl. (2024, 6 14). Retrieved from Alim.org: https://www.alim.org/history/prophet-companions/13/

14 Dawud, S. A. (2024, 7 18). Retrieved from Sunnah.com: https://sunnah.com/abudawud:2387

15 Evans, E. (2024, 2 29). 411 Rumi Quotes to Celebrate Life and Bring Contentment. Retrieved from Brightdrops: https://brightdrops.com/rumi-quotes

16 Ibid.

17 Sahih Muslim 285. (2024, 7 18). The Book of Purification. https://sunnah.com/muslim:285.

18 Majah, I. (2024, 7 18). The Book of Purification and its Sunnah. Retrieved from Sunnah.com: https://sunnah.com/ibnmajah:529

19 Rumi. (2024, 7 18). 37 Things Jalaluddin Rumi Can Teach You About Love. Retrieved from Purpose Fairy: https://purposefairy.com/85691/things-jalaluddin-rumi-teach-love.

20 Alim.org. (2024, 7 18). Retrieved from Alim.org: www.alim.org/history/prophet-companions/4/.

21 Sahih Muslim 2599. The Book of Virtue. sunnah.com/muslim:2599

22 Evans, E. (2024, 2 29). 411 Rumi Quotes to Celebrate Life and Bring Contentment. Retrieved from Brightdrops: https://brightdrops.com/rumi-quotes

23 The Concise Encyclopedia of Islam by Cyril Glasse, Page 141.

24 Attar. Trans. Fadiman and Robert Frager. Essential Sufism, page 118. Edison. Castle Books. 1997. 0785809066.

118

25 al-Bukhari, S. (2024, 9 5). Sahih al-Bukhari 3321. Retrieved from Sunnah.com: sunnah.com/bukhari:3321

26 From Hadith Qudsi #32, sunnah.com/qudsi40.

27 Sultan Bahu, translated by J. R. Puri and K. S. Khak page 358.

28 For example, humney likha (I wrote).

29 The Free Dictionary. [Online] [Cited: 8 16, 2017.] www.thefreedictionary.com/Pluralis+majestatis.

30 Rumi. Discourses of Rumi. Rumi [Online] [Cited: July 9, 3016.] www.rumi.org.uk/discourses.html

31 Evans, E. (2024, 2 29). 411 Rumi Quotes to Celebrate Life and Bring Contentment. Retrieved from Brightdrops: https://brightdrops.com/rumi-quotes

32 Mostafa, M. (2024, 2 29). Love in Islam. Retrieved from The Threshold Society: sufism.org/lineage/practice-and-adab/love-in-islam-2

33 Sahih Muslim 2564, sunnah.com/muslim:2564c

34 Evans, E. (2024, 2 29). 411 Rumi Quotes to Celebrate Life and Bring Contentment. Retrieved from Brightdrops: https://brightdrops.com/rumi-quotes

35 Haykal, Muhammad Husayn. Translated by I.R. al Faruqi, page 453. The life of Muhammad. New Delhi. Millat Book Center. 1976.

36 Taymiyyah, ibn. Being a True Slave of Allah. Aqeedah Of The Salaf AS-Salih [Online] [Cited: 7 9, 2016.] https://muslimscreed.wordpress.com/2011/12/07/being-a-true-slave-of-allah-by-shaykh-ul-islam-ibn-taymiyyah

37 893, Riyad . as-Salihin. (2014, 9 5). Retrieved from Sunnah.com: sunnah.com/riyadussalihin:893

38 Bukhari, no. 853 and Muslim, no. 1829. sunnah.com/abudawud:2928

39 Evans, E. (2024, 2 29). 411 Rumi Quotes to Celebrate Life and Bring Contentment. Retrieved from Brightdrops: https://brightdrops.com/rumi-quotes.

40 Encyclopaedia of Islam, Second Edition. Zulm. Brill Online [Online] [Cited: January 19, 2013.] http://referenceworks.brillonline.com/entries/encyclopaedia-of-islam-2/zulm-COM_1393.

41 Ibid.

42 Ibid.

43 Lane, E.W. Arabic-English Lexicon. London. Willams & Norgate,1863. 9780946621033

44 Dictionary of the Holy Quran by Abdul Mannan Omar page 351

45 " Ẓulm." Encyclopaedia of Islam, Second Edition. Brill Online , 2013. Reference. Eeshat Ansari. 19 January 2013 <http://referenceworks.brillonline.com/entries/encyclopaedia-of-islam-2/zulm-COM_1393>

46 Hadith Nawawi [# 24]

47 Bukhari. Book 2, Hadith 23 (2024, 7 21). Belief. Retrieved from https://sunnah.com/: https://sunnah.com/bukhari:30

48 al-Sheha Abdul-Rahma, Misconception on human rights on Islam, page 67-68. Riyadh.

49 Abdullah ibn Umm Maktum. (2024, 7 20). Retrieved from Alim.org: https://www.alim.org/history/prophet-companions/7/

50 Abu Yousuf. al-Kharaj. p.144 Quoted in Human Rights in Islam And Common Misconceptions by al-Sheha Abdul-Rahma.

51 Dargin, J. (2023, 3 10). Water Conservation in Islamic Teachings. Retrieved from https://www.ecomena.org/water-conservation-islam.

[52] Bukhari. Book 2, Hadith 23. (2024, 7 21). Belief. Retrieved from https://sunnah.com/: https://sunnah.com/bukhari:30.

[53] Tirmidhi quoted in Islamic Tahdhib and Akhlaq. P138 Lemu, Aisha. Chicago, IQRA International Educational Foundation. 2001. 1563163209.

[54] Bukhari, Hadith no. 3483, www.alim.org/hadith/sahih-bukhari/4/.

[55] Ibn Majah, Hadith no. 3172. https://sunnah.com/ibnmajah:3172

[56] Mariful Quran. English. 4:105. Page 565.

[57] Sahih Bukhari 5.701, quranx.com/hadith/Bukhari/USC-MSA/Volume-5/Book-59/Hadith-701/

[58] *Islamic Jurisprudence* is defined as the science which deals with observance of rituals, principles of the five pillars, and social legislation.

[59] Sahih Bukhari 2306 (2024,10,20). Retrieved from sunnah.com/bukhari:2306

[60] Zahoor, Akram. Muslim History 570 - 1950 CE. Gaithersburg, MD : 0-9702389-0-8, 2000.

[61] al-Mubarakpuri, S. R. (n.d.). The Sealed Nectar.

[62] Ibid.

[63] Hisham, S. I. (2000). Biography of the Prophet. Cairo: Al Falah Foundation.

[64] al-Mubarakpuri, S. R. (n.d.). The Sealed Nectar.

[65] The Prophet Muhammad: A Mercy for all Creation. www.islamweb.net [Online] [Cited: 1 1, 2017.] http://www.islamweb.net/en/article/134199/the-prophet-muhammad-a-mercy-for-all-creation.

[66] Barquera, R. &. (2024, 6 18). The secrets of Maya child sacrifice. Retrieved from The Conversation: https://theconversation.com/the-secrets-of-maya-child-sacrifice-at-chichen-itza-uncovered-using-ancient-dna-221610

[67] Bukhari. Alim CD, 3.778. quranx.com/Hadith/Bukhari/USC-MSA/Volume-3/Book-47/Hadith-778

[68] Kaylani, M.I. Jihad ke masail, Page 157, 159. Riyad, Maktaba Darussalam. 1999.

[69] Bukhari 5063, Book 67, Hadith 1. sunnah.com/bukhari:5063

[70] Bukhari 8.380, Volume 8, Book 75, quranx.com/hadith/Bukhari/USC-MSA/Volume-8/Book-75/Hadith-380/

[71] Abdul Malik Mujahid, Golden Stories of Umar Ibn Al-Khattab, p79, Darussalam Publishers, ASIN: B00DMI6XN0

[72] Chase-Dunn, C. Review of Ross Hassig, Aztec Warfare. The Institute for Research on World-Systems [Online] [Cited: July 24, 2016.] http://irows.ucr.edu/cd/bookrevs/hassig.txt.

[73] Shahi Bukhari 3.624. quranx.com/hadith/Bukhari/USC-MSA/Volume-3/Book-43/Hadith-624/

[74] Sahih al-Bukhari 2620 (2024, 10 17). Retrieved from Sunnah.com: sunnah.com/bukhari:2620

[75] Muslim 961b (2024, 10 17). Retrieved from Sunnah.com: sunnah.com/muslim:961b.

[76] Al-Halawani, A. (2024, 1 17). 9 Hadiths on How to Deal With Non-Muslims in Your Life. Retrieved from AboutIslam: aboutislam.net/shariah/hadith/hadith-collections/9-hadiths-show-deal-non-muslims-around/

[77] "Jihad in the Quran" by Louay Fatoohi page 37. Birmingham, Luna Plena Publishing. 2009. 9781906342067.

[78] Hamidullah, D. (1941). The First Written Constitution. Page 23,24.

[79] Maududi, A.A. Human rights in Islam. page 36,37,38. Narobi, The Islamic Foundation, 1990. 0950395498.

[80] Abu Dawud as quoted in Human rights in Islam p 36

81 Human rights in Islam by A. A. Maududi page 37

82 Prophet Muhammad's Last Sermon. IntroductionToISLAM.org. [Online] [Cited: 7 16, 2016.] http://www.introductiontoislam.org/prophetlastsermon.shtml.

83 Ahmad, A. B. (2004, Sept). Bilal bin Rabah. Retrieved from The Golden Series of the Prophet's Companions: kalamullah.com/Books/Bilal-bin-Rabah-The-Muadhdhin-Caller-to-Prayer.pdf

84 Ferguson, S. (2023, 9 1). What Can Cause or Contribute to Domestic Violence? Retrieved from healthline: www.healthline.com/health/causes-of-domestic-violence

85 Huecker, M. R., King, K. C., Jordan, G. A., & Smock, W. (2023, April 9). Domestic Violence. Retrieved from The National Center for Biotechnology Information: www.ncbi.nlm.nih.gov/books/NBK499891/

86 Sahih Muslim (2024, 10, 20). Retrieved from Sunnah.com: sunnah.com/muslim:2328a.

87 Vaughan-Lee, Llewellyn. Travelling the Path of Love: Sayings of Sufi Masters (p. 114). The Golden Sufi Center. Kindle Edition."

88 Mujahid, Abdul Malik. Ali (rta) vs. a Jew. Hiba [Online] [Cited: 1 23, 2017.] http://www.hibamagazine.com/ali-rta-vs-a-jew/.

89 Farooq, Mohammad Omar. Rape and Hudood Ordinance: Perversions of Justice in the Name of Islam. Social Science Research Network [Online] papers.ssrn.com/sol3/papers.cfm?abstract_id=1525412

90 Ibid

91 Tafseer Ibn Kathir, Urdu, Vol.3, Para 18, page 38. Delhi, Fareed Book Dept.

92 Farooq, Mohammad Omar. Rape and Hudood Ordinance: Perversions of Justice in the Name of Islam.

93 The Law, Patriarchy and Religious Fundamentalism- Women's Rights in Pakistan. Corrieri, Liliana. Hong Kong : Asian Legal Resource Center (AHLC), 2013. 978-962-8314-65-2

94 Farooq, Mohammad Omar. Rape and Hudood Ordinance: Perversions of Justice in the Name of Islam.

95 Alim.org-Al-Muwatta Hadith-15.41

96 Poliomyelitis. WHO [Online] [Cited: 1 4, 2017.] http://www.who.int/mediacentre/factsheets/fs114/en.

97 Bukhari 3.592. quranx.com/hadith/Bukhari/USC-MSA/Volume-3/Book-41/Hadith-592/

98 Vaughan-Lee, Llewellyn. Travelling the Path of Love: Sayings of Sufi Masters (p. 14). The Golden Sufi Center. Kindle Edition.

99 Muslim 910.

100 Bukhari 8.111. quranx.com/hadith/Bukhari/USC-MSA/Volume-8/Book-73/Hadith-111/

101 Ibn Taymiyyah quoted by Ibn ul Qayyim, Madaarij as-Saalikeen (The State of Repentance).

102 Evans, E. (2024, 2 29). 411 Rumi Quotes to Celebrate Life and Bring Contentment. Retrieved from Brightdrops: https://brightdrops.com/rumi-quotes

103 Al-Dawoody, Ahmed. The Islamic Law of War: Justifications and Regulations. Page 56. New York : PALGRAVE MACMILLAN, 2011. 978-0-230-11160-8.

104 Ashraf, S.M., Studies in Muslim Philosophy page 2. Lahore, 1997, 9694321565.

105 Herschensohn, Bruce. Across the Taiwan Strait: the bridge between mainland China and Taiwan. page 23. Lexington Books. 2002. 0739103423.

106 Ibn Kathir. Life of the Prophet Muhammad.

107 Depending upon the state.

108 al-Mubarakpuri, S. R. (n.d.). The Sealed Nectar.

109 Ibid.

[110] Zahoor, A. (2000). Muslim History 570 - 1950. Gaithersburg.

[111] Sahih Bukhari 5.619.

[112] Ali, Geragh. A Critical Exposition Of The Popular Jihad. Page iii. Dodo Press. 9781406568301.

[113] Fatoohi, Louay. Jihad in the Quran. page 34.

[114] Lewis, Bernard, Arabs in History. p. 57. Oxford University Press, 2002. 9780191587665.

[115] Naipaul, VS. Among the Believers. Page 82. Vintage. 1982. 0394711955.

[116] www.alim.org/library/quran/surah/introduction/48/QSI

[117] Lings, Martin. Muhammad. s.l. : Inner Traditions International, 1983. 0-89281-170-6. Page 248.

[118] Mariful Quran. English. 48:1-3. Vol. 8, Page 75.

[119] Ibid.

[120] Ibid.

[121] Ibid.

[122] Saifur Rahman al-Mubarakpuri, Ar-Raheeq Al-Makhtum (The Sealed Nectar), page 216.

[123] Mariful Quran. English. 48:1-3. Vol. 8, Page 77.

[124] Saifur Rahman al-Mubarakpuri, Ar-Raheeq Al-Makhtum (The Sealed Nectar), page 218.

[125] Al-Bouti, D. M. (2024, 11 9). Indeed, We Have Given You a Clear Victory. Retrieved from Islamonline: islamonline.net/en/the-treaty-of-hudaybiyyah/

[126] Haykal, M. (n.d.). page 136, The Life of Muhammad. New Delhi, India: Millat Book Center.

[127] Saifur Rahman al-Mubarakpuri, Ar-Raheeq Al-Makhtum (The Sealed Nectar), page 64.

[128] Ibid

[129] Mishra, K. (2017, Sept 6). Then Why Call Him God? Retrieved from Indian Economy and Market: https://indianeconomyandmarket.com/2017/09/06/then-why-call-him-god/

[130] Haykal, Muhammad Husayn. Translated by I.R. al Faruqi, page 453. The life of Muhammad. New Delhi. Millat Book Center. 1976.

[131] (2024, 5 12). Retrieved from HadeethEnc.com: hadeethenc.com/en/browse/hadith/6406

[132] Saifur Rahman al-Mubarakpuri, Ar-Raheeq Al-Makhtum.

[133] Ibid

[134] IslamFYI. (2017, 6 2). What does Islam actually mean? Retrieved from ISLAMFYI: islamfyi.princeton.edu/what-does-islam-actually-mean/

[135] Rayhan, A. (n.d.). In RUMI A JOURNEY THROUGH LOVE AND POETRY. Page 36, 37

[136] Witteveen, H. (2023, 12 31). Hazrat Inayat Khan Quotes. Retrieved from Goodreads: www.goodreads.com/quotes/tag/hazrat-inayat-khan#

[137] Evans, E. (2024, 2 29). 411 Rumi Quotes to Celebrate Life and Bring Contentment. Retrieved from Brightdrops: https://brightdrops.com/rumi-quotes

[138] Ahmad, S. F. (2014). GOD, ISLAM & THE SKEPTIC MIND: A Study on Faith, Science, Religious Diversity, Ethics, and Evil. ISBN: 9781497360020

[139] Habib, Z. (2021, 4 15). Dhikr - Remembrance of Allah. Retrieved from Farhat Hashmi: https://www.farhathashmi.com/articles-section/remembrance/dhikr-remembrance-of-allah

[140] Ibid.

[141] Vaughan-Lee, Llewellyn. Travelling the Path of Love: Sayings of Sufi Masters (p. 41). The Golden Sufi Center. Kindle Edition.

[142] Rabia Basri. (n.d.). Retrieved from AZQuotes: www.azquotes.com/quote/593732

[143] Evans, E. (2024, 2 29). 411 Rumi Quotes to Celebrate Life and Bring Contentment. Retrieved from Brightdrops: brightdrops.com/rumi-quotes

[144] Usmani, Shafi. English-MaarifulQuran – Volume 2. Page 250. s.l. : Maktaba-e-Darul Uloom.

[145] Sahih Bukhari Volume 1, Book 2, Hadith 39

[146] Rumi. (n.d.). ezquptes. Retrieved from www.azquotes.com/quote/752181#google_vignette

[147] Frohman, D. (n.d.). Retrieved from lawhimsy.com/2018/09/17/monday-mantra-218-your-wound-is-probably-not-your-fault-but-your-healing-is-your-responsibility/

[148] Evans, E. (2024, 2 29). 411 Rumi Quotes to Celebrate Life and Bring Contentment. Retrieved from Brightdrops: https://brightdrops.com/rumi-quotes

[149] Top 50 Ibn Qayyim Al-Jawziyya Quotes. (n.d.). Retrieved from quotefancy: quotefancy.com/ibn-qayyim-al-jawziyya-quotes

[148] Plato. (n.d.). Retrieved from Goodreads: www.goodreads.com/quotes/632075-those-who-are-able-to-see-beyond-the-shadows-and

www.ingramcontent.com/pod-product-compliance
Lightning Source LLC
Chambersburg PA
CBHW072354090426
42741CB00012B/3030